CALACH

CALACH

SANDRA K. JOHNSTON PHD, LP

TATE PUBLISHING
AND ENTERPRISES, LLC

Published by Tate Publishing & Enterprises, LLC
127 E. Trade Center Terrace | Mustang, Oklahoma 73064 USA
1.888.361.9473 | www.tatepublishing.com

Tate Publishing is committed to excellence in the publishing industry. The company reflects the philosophy established by the founders, based on Psalm 68:11,

"The Lord gave the word and great was the company of those who published it."

Book design copyright © 2015 by Tate Publishing, LLC. All rights reserved.
Cover design by Bill Francis Peralta
Interior design by Manolito Bastasa

Published in the United States of America

ISBN: 978-1-68164-662-6
1. Religion / Christian Ministry / Counseling & Recovery
2. Psychology / Psychotherapy / Counseling
15.07.09

CONTENTS

PREFACE

MY INTEREST IN the study and teaching forgiveness was purely accidental in human terms. For more than a decade, I have read and studied forgiveness research and have carried out my own research projects. The secular forgiveness research actually encouraged me to incorporate forgiveness in my psychotherapy practice since it supports God's Word. The life experiences, forgiveness battles, and successes of my clients have motivated me to write this material and to provide guidelines for others to understand both the spiritual and secular aspects of forgiveness. Needless to say, there is much confusion about forgiveness in the world. Everyone has a personal definition of forgiveness, which is often erroneous and passed from generation to generation. It is vital to have an accurate definition of forgiveness to be a successful forgiver. There are more than one hundred entries in the Bible about forgiveness according to Strong (2010).

Please be aware that the topic of forgiveness can stir up emotional responses that are uncomfortable. When completing the exercises, invite a trusted friend or family member to be with you if you believe you might need support. The material in this text is not intended to retraumatize anyone but to clarify, define, support, encourage, and perhaps bring healing. This also brings me to an important point. This material can be read and the exercises completed individually, but meeting with a group can be even more inspiring. As long as you can trust the group members and you make a rule to keep everything discussed confidential, the forgiveness exercises at the end of the text can create surprising results. The English Standard Version of scripture is used throughout this text.

1

God, the Great Psychotherapist

A-B-C: Affect, Behavior, Cognition

FORGIVENESS HAS BEEN relegated to the religious community throughout history. In the twenty-first century, it has been addressed by the secular scientific world as well. Psychotherapists began investigating the possibility of incorporating forgiveness into their treatment practices about seventy years ago. Today, forgiveness is emerging as a viable evidence-based, stand-alone treatment modality. Its foundations lie in the treatment modalities that have preceded it. Forgiveness is not a behavior or an emotion. It is the result of conscious thought and decision-making processes. Beliefs influence thoughts, which then influence behaviors and emotions, indicating that forgiveness therapy has a basis in cognitive theory. This chapter will address the foundations of therapy methods, which are employed in the forgiveness process, and will conclude with a more detailed explanation of forgiveness as a therapeutic tool.

God, the creator, made us in his image with emotions, actions, and thoughts. In psychotherapy terms, they are represented as the A-B-C model. Emotions are referred to as *affect*. Actions are referred to as *behaviors*. Thoughts are referred to as *cognitions*. Affect is the ability to feel, emote, and outwardly express the sensations that one experiences internally. Behavior is action in outward expression through mannerisms on the physical level. It includes any active response to the environment or to stimuli in the environment; it is an exhibition of sorts. Cognitions are the product of mental activity and include acquired knowledge, reasoning, imagining, reflection, recollection, meditation, contemplation, perception, intuition, and intention. God gave mankind proprietary authority over affect, behavior, and cognition, which is the choice to express each of them at will. On the other hand, they have the ability to control an individual as well. That struggle between either controlling affect, behaviors, and thoughts, or being controlled by them is the basis for the study and practice of psychology.

This opening chapter will address each of these three areas from biblical and secular points of view. First, for each factor listed (affect, behavior, cognition), scriptures will be provided that declare what the Word of God says about each domain followed by an explanatory thesis of the current psychological theory on the matter as well as the current treatment that is resultant of the theory and theorist. Lastly, a summary comparison of the scriptural and secular methods will be provided.

What God Says about Affect

God is a being who has and displays emotions, and having been created in his image, it naturally follows that we have those same emotions. The Bible indicates that God and Jesus are attributed with emotions, which we generally believe are only human reactions. Not only are their emotions recorded for us in scripture, but also the intensity of those emotions displayed by both God and Jesus. The following examples illustrate this point.

Jesus wept. (John 11:35)

For we do not have a high priest who is unable to sympathize with our weaknesses, but one who in every respect has been tempted as we are, yet without sin. (Heb. 4:15)

May the God of hope fill you with all joy and peace in believing, so that by the power of the Holy Spirit you may abound in hope. (Rom. 15:13)

Arise, O Lord, in your anger; lift yourself up against the fury of my enemies; awake for me; you have appointed a judgment. (Ps. 7:6)

The range of emotions human beings are capable of sensing and displaying incorporates the possible responses to every emotion ignited by every possible life event or circumstance. Secular researchers have recently decided that there are only four basic emotions: happy, sad, afraid/surprised, and angry/disgusted (Jack, Garrod, and Schyns 2014). They make this determination based upon the expressions of the human face, which is also found in the scriptures.

A glad heart makes a cheerful face, but by sorrow of heart the spirit is crushed. (Prov. 15:13)

This research indicates that scientists have determined that all other emotions arise from, or are simply other forms of, those four basic emotions. Based upon my experience as a practitioner of psychology and not simply as a researcher, I would challenge the researchers to add two more emotions: tenderness or love and peacefulness or contentedness.

Both of those emotions can also be seen in facial expressions particularly the expression in the eyes. Thus, I will address six emotions, and for the purposes of this book, I will refer to the emotions mentioned in scripture as happiness (joy), tenderness (love), peace (contentedness), sadness, anger, and fear. The only emotion God does not share with mankind is fear. The only time in scripture that fear is mentioned in conjunction with the Trinity is the anticipatory fear Jesus Christ felt in the garden of Gethsemane prior to his crucifixion. God has directed us to control our emotions and provides examples of emotions throughout his word through examples of the negative and positive consequences of responding to each.

Happiness

> These things I have spoken to you, that my joy may be in you, and that your joy may be full. (John 15:11)

> Until now you have asked nothing in my name. Ask, and you will receive, that your joy may be full. (John 16:24)

> May the God of hope fill you with all joy and peace in believing, so that by the power of the Holy Spirit you may abound in hope. (Rom. 15:13)

Love

> Since you are precious in My sight, Since you are honored and I love you, I will give other men in your place and other peoples in exchange for your life. (Isa. 43:4)

> Beloved, let us love one another, for love is from God, and whoever loves has been born of God and knows God. (1 John 4:7)

> Hatred stirs up strife, but love covers all offenses. (Prov. 10:12)

Peace

> You keep him in perfect peace whose mind is stayed on you, because he trusts in you. (Isa. 26:3)

> And the peace of God, which surpasses all understanding, will guard your hearts and your minds in Christ Jesus. (Phil. 4:7)

> The Lord appeared to him from afar, saying, "I have loved you with an everlasting love; Therefore I have drawn you with lovingkindness. (Jer. 31:3)

Fear

For God did not give us a spirit not of fear but of power and love and self-control. (2 Tim. 1:7)

Fear not, for I am with you; be not dismayed, for I am your God; I will strengthen you, I will help you, I will uphold you with my righteous right hand. (Isa. 41:10)

When I am afraid, I put my trust in you. In God, whose word I praise, in God I trust; I shall not be afraid. What can flesh do to me? (Ps. 56:3–4)

There is no fear in love, but perfect love casts out fear. For fear has to do with punishment, and whoever fears has not been perfected in love. (1 John 4:18)

Even though I walk through the valley of the shadow of death, I will fear no evil, for you are with me; your rod and your staff, they comfort me. (Ps. 23:4)

Rejoice in the Lord always; again I will say, Rejoice. Let your reasonableness be known to everyone. The

Lord is at hand; do not be anxious about anything, but in everything by prayer and supplication with thanksgiving let your requests be made known to God. And the peace of God, which surpasses all understanding, will guard your hearts and your minds in Christ Jesus. (Phil. 4:4–7)

Sadness

For godly grief produces a repentance that leads to salvation without regret, whereas worldly grief produces death. (2 Cor. 7:10)

Why are you cast down, O my soul, and why are you in turmoil within me? Hope in God; for I shall again praise him, my salvation and my God. (Ps. 43:5)

He will wipe away every tear from their eyes, and death shall be no more, neither shall there be mourning, nor crying, nor pain anymore, for the former things have passed away. (Rev. 21:4)

Anger

> Whoever is slow to anger is better than the mighty, and he who rules his spirit than he who takes a city. (Prov. 16:32)

> The vexation of a fool is known at once, but the prudent ignores an insult. (Prov. 12:16)

> Be angry and do not sin; do not let the sun go down on your anger, and give no opportunity to the devil. (Eph. 4:26–27)

Secular Methods for Dealing with Emotional Struggles

Many individuals with issues that are based on emotional dysregulation have specific vulnerability and heightened intensity of response to external stimuli. This may be due to a lack of clear identity formation or, to put it another way, may not have continuity of personality development. Each person feels emotions at a different level at different times and based upon differing sets of criteria. What makes one person angry may not make another person angry. What makes one person happy may not make another person happy. Or both may be happy at differing levels of intensity. Take for instance Christmas morning. Two individuals in the same family may have two very different responses to the traditional family get-together. One person may be joyfully looking forward to seeing relatives she hasn't seen in a year, and the other family member may be only mildly happy about interacting with the family because she does not have the same sense of intimacy with them. Some individuals are so controlled by their emotional responses that they cannot regulate them or turn them on or off. They feel like they are drowning in a sea of pain, or they may feel incredibly invincible. In this instance, without learning and practicing healthy coping skills, the results can be potentially disastrous. There is a psychotherapy that addresses inappropriate levels of emotional response. The name of that modality is Dialectical Behavior Therapy or DBT.

Dialectical Behavior Therapy (DBT)

Marsha M. Linehan is the founder of Dialectical Behavior Therapy (DBT). It was developed in response to suicidal and self-harm behaviors of clients living with severe personality disorders (Linehan 1993). One of the initial goals of the treatment was validation or normalization of client's thoughts, feelings, and behaviors. Many clients have no sense of themselves in that they are constantly feeling intrapersonal uncertainty and failure. The four modules of DBT are mindfulness (based on Buddhist mindfulness meditation), distress tolerance, emotion regulation, and interpersonal effectiveness.

The key difference between DBT and other forms of behavior therapy is the focus on emotion regulation. This is accomplished through detailed client recordings of emotionally intense events. Techniques are similar to those used in cognitive therapy, only they are applied to emotions instead of thoughts and include emotion awareness, emotion evaluation, emotion, stopping, emotion replacement, acceptance of emotions, letting go of emotions. Although it was not originally designed to treat mania, the protocol can be adapted to help individuals with bipolar mania recognize their triggers, be mindful of the patterns that lead to manic episodes, and regulate their feelings. The empirically sound research on the effectiveness of DBT is weak, but proponents claim that it has a high success rate with certain behavioral health populations.

Summary of Scripture and Emotions

How does science support scripture when it comes to emotional health? Research indicates that emotional health impacts physical health as well. Negative emotions can make a person physically ill (Kubzansky and Kawachi 2000) while positive emotions increase overall well-being (Tugade, Fredrickson, and Feldman-Barrett 2004). Scriptures clearly point out that anxiety, worry, fear, and sorrow cause not only emotional suffering but physical suffering as well. Science does not contradict the Bible in any of these matters. Emotional health is also closely tied to behaviors and their consequences.

What God Says about Behavior

The most obvious topic of behavior that comes to mind when we think about the Bible is the topic of sin or disobedience. The scriptures are full of actions that prevent us from having eternal life, that hurt us, or that hurt others. The God who created us also understands that mankind has limited capabilities and that although we have both good and bad human characteristics, one or the other will dominate; in particular, the original sin nature that is without God. The following are a few of the many scriptures reminding us that mankind fell from grace.

Sin

> For all have sinned and fall short of the glory of God. (Rom. 3:23)

No servant can serve two masters, for either he will hate the one and love the other, or he will be devoted to the one and despise the other. You cannot serve God and money. (Luke 16:13)

Or do you not know that the unrighteous will not inherit the kingdom of God? Do not be deceived: neither the sexually immoral, nor idolaters, nor adulterers, nor men who practice homosexuality, nor thieves, nor the greedy, nor drunkards, nor revilers, nor swindlers will inherit the kingdom of God. And such were some of you. But you were washed, you were sanctified, you were justified in the name of the Lord Jesus Christ and by the Spirit of our God. (1 Cor. 6:9–11)

Put to death therefore what is earthly in you: sexual immorality, impurity, passion, evil desire, and covetousness, which is idolatry. (Col. 3:5)

Training us to renounce ungodliness and worldly passions, and to live self-controlled, upright, and godly lives in the present age. (Titus 2:12)

But Peter and the apostles answered, "We must obey God rather than men." (Acts 5:29)

The scriptures also specify what constitutes good or appropriate behavior and the positive results of obedience to God. God does not want to condemn us. He wants us to be socially proactive helping others, be socially responsible, and also care for ourselves. These behaviors are referred to as life-giving rather than leading to physical and spiritual death. They are the basis for ethical and moral behavior. God, who created us, also knows what will hurt us. Even when we believe we are doing the right thing at times, the end result may be emptiness, loss, or immediate or delayed pain. God responds by revealing to us the behaviors that will help us be successful and meet our goals. God's word on behavior is comprehensive.

Success

> Therefore be imitators of God, as beloved children. And walk in love, as Christ loved us and gave himself up for us, a fragrant offering and sacrifice to God. (Eph. 5:1–2)

> By this my Father is glorified, that you bear much fruit and so prove to be my disciples. (John 15:8)

> But the fruit of the Spirit is love, joy, peace, patience, kindness, goodness, faithfulness, gentleness, self-

control; against such things there is no law. (Gal 5:22–23)

Therefore a man shall leave his father and his mother and hold fast to his wife, and they shall become one flesh. (Gen. 2:24)

Behavior Toward God's Creation

God even desires that we treat his creation (nature and animals) with respect, dignity, and compassion. God mentions the heavens, constellations, stars, and planets in his word and how they point to his incredible creative skill. According to scripture, he also has a close relationship with the flora he created (see verses below). He refers to it as pleasant repeatedly, and in return, all nature glorifies and praises him through its very existence. Animals are important to God. He allows man to eat meat, but he wants us to care for all animals and treat them with respect and dignity.

The heavens declare the glory of God, and the sky above proclaims his handiwork. (Ps. 19:1)

And God saw everything that he had made, and behold, it was very good. And there was evening and there was morning, the sixth day. (Gen. 1:31)

And out of the ground the Lord God made to spring up every tree that is pleasant to the sight and good for food. (Gen. 2:9)

Let the rivers clap their hands; let the hills sing for joy together. (Ps. 98:8)

Whoever is righteous has regard for the life of his beast, but the mercy of the wicked is cruel. (Prov. 12:10)

If you meet your enemy's ox or his donkey going astray, you shall bring it back to him. If you see the donkey of one who hates you lying down under its burden, you shall refrain from leaving him with it; you shall rescue it with him. (Exod. 23:4–5)

Behavior toward God

The scriptures are also replete with examples of our expected behavior toward God. He teaches us about how he wants us to treat him, although we still have the choice whether or not we will do so. This is what makes Christianity different from other religions. God desires a dynamic, symbiotic relationship with us as intimate as the relationship between a husband and a wife or a parent and a beloved child. He desires our unsolicited praise and worship. He desires a love relationship that we willingly enter with him.

> He answered, "I tell you, if these [people] were silent, the very stones would cry out. (Luke 19:40)

> Praise the Lord! Praise God in his sanctuary; praise him in his mighty heavens! Praise him for his mighty deeds; praise him according to his excellent greatness! Praise him with trumpet sound; praise him with lute and harp! Praise him with tambourine and dance; praise him with strings and pipe! Praise him with sounding cymbals; praise him with loud clashing cymbals! (Ps. 150:1–6)

Now let us investigate what secular psychologists have hypothesized and/or discovered about human behavior. The following is an explanatory expository of man's view of mankind and man's theory of human behavior. Research not only provides material for critical thinking, but even supports God's knowledge of sin and its consequences versus good or healthy behavior and its positive consequences.

Behavior Therapy (BT)

B. F. Skinner is the man we think of as the father of operant conditioning and is associated with pure behavior therapy. It is by far the most scientific of all forms of psychotherapy, adhering to the most stringent experimental protocol including identifying the target behavior, defining a hypothesis about the behavioral pattern, identifying change motivators, establishing a baseline for the target behavior, establishing meaningful measurement of the target behavior, and training the client to eventually perform those tasks for her/himself. Behavior therapy purists focus solely on the behavioral response of the individual without consideration for thoughts or emotions. The mind is considered an inaccessible black box, which cannot be understood. In other words, the client does not need insight, awareness, or understanding of the problem for change to occur.

This purely scientific viewpoint of humankind arose from Skinner's ideology that we are both the products and producers of our environment (Corey 2009). We act (behave) on the environment, and in turn, the environment acts (behaves) on us. This expository reciprocal relationship of stimulus-response feedback loops shapes what we become and how we will behave in the future. The individual is not considered a personality but is seen as the culmination of behavior patterns. The behavior that is addressed for the purpose of change is called the target behavior.

Motivation is all that is needed to produce change in the form of reinforcement (either positive or negative) or punishment (either positive or negative). A motivator that increases a behavior is considered reinforcement. Any motivator that decreases a behavior is considered punishment. A positive consequence indicates that something is added to the individual while a negative consequence indicates that something is removed from the individual. A clear picture emerges in the table below. Examples are provided to improve the reader's understanding of the process.

	Behavior Increases	Behavior Decreases
Stimulus Applied	Positive Reinforcement	Positive Punishment
Stimulus Removed	Negative Reinforcement	Negative Punishment

An example of positive reinforcement is the praise and a raise you receive from your boss when you have done a good job. The praise and increased salary are added to you and tend to increase the behavior for which you are being rewarded. This is the strongest of all forms of behavior change. An example of negative reinforcement is the annoying sound your car emits when you have not fastened your seat belt. The sound motivates you to fasten your seat belt, thus increasing your behavior via something that is unpleasant but is for your safety. Once you perform the target behavior, the unpleasant sound stops. Positive punishment is the application of something unpleasant that is applied to the individual, such as spanking a child. It is meant to decrease a particular action or behavior through the addition of the unpleasant sensation. It can be the least effective type of behavior modification if used too frequently. For example, children who are physically punished on a daily basis simply become bitter and adapt to the punishment, thus making it ineffective. The goal of negative punishment is to reduce or eliminate a behavior by removing something reinforcing from the individual, such as taking away TV privileges from an adolescent until her/his homework is completed.

Obviously, the process of changing behavior that is deemed unhealthy, dangerous, or not beneficial to society or the individual relies solely on addressing observable behavior/s. It is much like training an animal. When one wants a response from a rat, for example, one discovers what motivates the rat to perform a certain action. It may be a positive reward for performing an action such as food, or it may be avoidance of a punishment such as fleeing the portion of the cage in which electric shocks are given.

The ability of the researcher or therapist to first discover the basic behavior that is the target of change is key. Next, factors that motivate the individual to change are recorded. Then a baseline behavior measurement is taken so that levels of improvement can be tracked. A schedule is created of the target behavior in the presence or absence of the motivating factor. Behavior therapists spend considerable amounts of time measuring the changes in behavior by which to determine with as much accuracy as possible whether or not the treatment is working via the motivating factors. Throughout this process, the client is also learning how to employ this method when not in the presence of the therapist.

The therapist emphasizes teaching and self-management in the individually tailored treatment plan. So there is an element of conditioning or learning that takes place simply by the therapist directing the client to keep track of specific behaviors and their frequency and how to administer the rewards or punishments. In the case of shaping the behavior of a child, the parent learns over time to not only shape the child's behavior, but also how to become an amateur (if you will) behavior therapist.

The above is indicative of the collaborative, active role that both the therapist and the client take in treatment. The client's past is of little value except for establishing the motivators that led to the current behavior. The current issues are the focus rather than correcting forces of the past, which may or may not be present in the here and now.

Current behavior therapy includes sensitivity to cultural dynamics within the environment, which also produce the behavior the client exhibits. This does not mean that excuses are made for the client but that all factors must be taken into consideration for the treatment plan to be effective. There is also an emphasis on development of problem-solving skills that can apply in the most challenging situations for the client, making behavior therapy a successful modality in prisons, schools, and places of employment as well as home environments. Behavior therapy increases the personal choice of the client to help tailor the individual treatment plan to the environmental, social, political factors, including issues of potential discrimination. Therefore, the goals of behavior therapy are central to successful outcomes. To be of scientific value as well, they must be clear, concise, practical, and concrete.

The functional assessment model (FAM) uses all the information gathered about the client to define the target behavior, create a hypothesis about the behavior, and devise a treatment plan. Once a treatment plan has been written, the client uses a log or diary to keep track of the number of occurrences of the target behavior, such as the number of cigarettes smoked each day for thirty days. Having taken a baseline of the target behavior prior to the implementation or introduction of the motivating factor/s provides the therapist with evidence of whether or not the treatment is effective. In fact, the behavior log can be quite detailed and specific as to time of day, environmental stressors that are present, the place the behavior occurs, who is present when the behavior occurs, and the direct consequence of the behavior in the presence of the reward or punishment. Information gathered from the client logs is reevaluated by the therapist and client frequently so that alterations in the plan can be made regularly as needed. This is another reminder that the relationship between the therapist and the client is collaborative, active, and directive to allow change to occur.

Summary of Scripture versus Behavior Therapy

God's view of man's actions is similar to the behavior theorists' views in that there are consequences or rewards and punishments for every action. The consequences may occur naturally in the environment, or they may be impugned by other people. God knows that human beings have the capacity to repeat actions that bring negative consequences on themselves and on others. While the behaviorists initially thought that an action that brought pleasant results would be repeated while an action that produced unpleasant results would not be repeated, eventually they came to realize that was not true (Thorndike 1911). Human beings will continue to exhibit behaviors that have negative consequences to the point of total destruction of life as the Bible also depicts.

A well-known story occurred between Saul and David. The pressures of being king greatly weighed upon Saul. According to scripture, he began experiencing anxiety and paranoia to the point of delusional thinking. Emotional and mental health issues are evident in modern rulers as well and have even been highly publicized in some instances. In an effort to help calm King Saul, David was hired to play music to distract Saul from his mental anguish. Music for the purpose of relaxation is a common psychotherapy method used even today. In the end, Saul's paranoia grew so intense that he believed David was his enemy. He began to try to kill David. David, on the other hand, continued to forgive Saul and seek ways to ward him off without killing him. In the end, Saul was destroyed by his increasingly violent behavior. David exercised self-control and became king over Israel. This story clearly depicts the value of healthy behaviors versus the consequences of negative behaviors.

The problem with the secular view is that pure behavior theory does not hold human beings responsible for their actions in the same way that God does. Behavior theory states that humans are more like robots that are programmed by the environment simply by the reward/punishment process. Behavior theory does not address free will nor does it find that man can make conscious choices to change through insight. God's word indicates that we are consciously responsible for our actions since they impact the environment. We are therefore urged to be socially responsible, spiritually aware, and learn from our mistakes as well as our successes.

What God Says about Cognitions

God wrote about thoughts long before man studied them or developed theories about them. Man was not created to dwell on negative thoughts which cause us to become fearful, angry, and depressed. The Bible is replete with verses that address our thought life and how to handle it. First, God knew that we would wage a war with negative thoughts whether they are inappropriate, self-defeating, manipulative, etc.

> Finally, brothers, whatever is true, whatever is honorable, whatever is just, whatever is pure, whatever is lovely, whatever is commendable, if there is any excellence, if there is anything worthy of praise, think about these things. (Phil. 4:8)

In the previous verse, there is an implication that we can consciously stop negative thoughts and replace them with those that are positive. Scripture also gives us a protocol or pattern to follow, indicating which thoughts are more beneficial to us and lead to life rather than death; spiritual and emotional life versus spiritual and emotional death. The following verses indicate God's plan for identifying or recognizing negative thoughts and the consequences of giving in to them.

Negative thinking

> But watch yourselves lest your hearts be weighed down with dissipation and drunkenness and cares of this life, and that day come upon you suddenly like a trap. (Luke 21:34)

> But I see in my members another law waging war against the law of my mind and making me captive to the law of sin that dwells in my members. (Rom. 7:23)

> He is a double-minded man, unstable in all his ways. (James 1:8)

We are directed to transform or renew our minds, and then God moves our thoughts in a positive direction. The following verses define God's plan for stopping, challenging, and replacing negative thoughts with positive thoughts before they get out of hand.

Positive thinking

> Do not be conformed to this world, but be transformed by the renewal of your mind, that by testing you may discern what is the will of God, what is good and acceptable and perfect. (Rom. 12:2)

> We destroy arguments and every lofty opinion raised against the knowledge of God, and take every thought captive to obey Christ, being ready to punish every disobedience, when your obedience is complete. (2 Cor. 10:5–6)

> If then you have been raised with Christ, seek the things that are above, where Christ is, seated at the right hand of God. Set your minds on things that are above, not on things that are on earth. (Col. 3:1–2)

You keep him in perfect peace whose mind is stayed on you, because he trusts in you. (Isa. 26:3)

And he said to him, "You shall love the Lord your God with all your heart and with all your soul and with all your mind." (Matt. 22:37)

Thanks be to God through Jesus Christ our Lord! So then, I myself serve the law of God with my mind, but with my flesh I serve the law of sin. (Rom. 7:25)

God also assures us that we can make a choice to think positive thoughts, which will benefit us in the following ways: (1) we will strengthen our own faith and accomplish more, and (2) release him to work on our behalf. The woman in the verses below did just that. Her need was so great that she let go of all negative thoughts and focused only on her goal. She did not focus on the illness or on breaking a Jewish law by being unclean in a public venue, but on her healing.

And behold, a woman who had suffered from a discharge of blood for twelve years came up behind him and touched the fringe of his garment, for she said to herself, "If I only touch his garment, I will be made well." Jesus turned, and seeing her he said,

"Take heart, daughter; your faith has made you well." And instantly the woman was made well. (Matt. 9:20–22)

Finally, God tells us what his thoughts are toward us (Ps. 139:17; Ps. 115:9). God does not waste time ruminating about issues. He has forgiven us, cast our sins far from us so that he remembers them no more (Ps. 103:12, Heb. 8:12), and totally accepts us through Jesus' death on the cross. Since we are created in his image, we have the power to give up ruminating as well and focus our minds on higher and loftier things. Secular scientists have developed methods for doing exactly what God has directed us to do. They are grouped under the domain of cognitive therapies.

Cognitive Therapy (CT)

While behavior therapy only focuses on behavior and denies the presence of thoughts or emotions, cognitive therapists believe that cognitions cannot be separated from the person (Corey 2009). Cognitive theory states that the mind is not a mysterious, unknowable black box but that thoughts influence behaviors. Humans are not on the same level with animals but at a higher level of functioning in which not only do we have thoughts, but we also have metacognition—the ability to have thoughts about thoughts (Kalish and Lawson 2007). From those assumptions arose a number of thought-based theories and clinical practices.

Cognitive therapists focus on identification of negative thoughts, stopping negative thoughts or thought patterns, challenging negative thoughts, and replacing negative thoughts with more positive thoughts.

Rational Emotive Behavior Therapy (REBT)

Albert Ellis was an American psychologist and the father of Rational Emotive Behavior Therapy (REBT). He believed that people contribute to their own psychological problems and specific symptoms by the way they interpret and think about the world (Corey 2005). Ellis also believed that we learn negative self-talk from others in childhood but that it is our own responsibility for perpetuating them into adulthood. He theorized that individuals have innate rational (self- and socially-constructive) and irrational (self- and socially-destructive) tendencies. Ellis (2003) purported that insight into ourselves and our problems was necessary for change to occur, unlike behavior theory.

His goal was to teach his clients to separate the evaluation of their behaviors from the evaluation of themselves, and in so doing, to create new emotions and behaviors in the client. Take note that Ellis honored his clients by assuming that they had the ability to control their thoughts about life events rather than trying to control the event or being controlled by the event.

He stated that thoughts, feelings, and actions were intricately related to one another and affected one another (Ellis 2003). Ellis developed the ABCDE model (not to be confused with the A-B-Cs mentioned at the outset of this chapter) which addressed the cognitive absolutes (should, must, ought) that unnecessarily burden individuals. The following example will clarify the theoretical concept.

A = activating event (usually something we perceive as negative)

B = belief about the event (whether it is supported by facts)

C = consequence of the belief about the event (our response and results of it)

D = dispute the irrational thought (changing the way we think about the event)

E = effective new belief

Activating event	Belief	Consequence	Dispute	Effective new belief
Someone called me a bad name	"People *should* respect me."	Anger	"Does anyone really *have* to respect me?"	"People don't really *have* to respect me."
	"It is *horrible* to be disrespected."	Shame	"How bad is this on a scale of 0–100? Is there anything worse than this?"	"I don't like this situation, but there are worse things."

	"That person is rude and evil for treating me that way!"	Hatred	"Is it sensible to expect this person to act as I want them to?"	"This person is a fallible human being like everyone else, and is not totally bad."

The point of changing our beliefs and thinking patterns is to relieve the suffering that we experience when we believe negative thoughts about our circumstances, others, or ourselves. In the above example, *should* or *horrible* becomes a burden that is too hard to bear. The effective new beliefs in the last column allow for differences of opinion between people without judging that either party is right or wrong. Your thoughts do not have to be controlled by the beliefs someone else holds about you.

Cognitive Behavioral Therapy (CBT)

About the same time that Ellis was developing REBT, American psychiatrist Aaron T. Beck was developing Cognitive Behavioral Therapy (CBT). Beck's approach, unlike Ellis's, did not view people as irrational beings but, like REBT, deemed insight necessary for change (Corsini and Wedding 2010). He developed cognitive behavioral therapy to treat depressive symptoms that arose from perfectionistic, rigid, core beliefs (schemas, cognitive distortions, or thinking errors). Beck (2009) believed that self-talk was critical for self-understanding and could be blocked in some individuals by distorted thoughts. Awareness of thinking errors allows an individual the ability to pause, reevaluate, and rethink a negative schema then replace it with one that is more positive.

Schema/ Thinking Errors	Explanation	Example
Arbitrary inferences	Making a judgment with no supporting inferences	Believing someone does not like you without any actual information to support the belief
Overgeneralization	Making a broad rule with little support	Believing that if an exam went badly, all of them will
Catastrophizing	Blowing something out of proportion	Believing that one minor mistake will ruin your entire life
Labeling/ mislabeling	Attaching a negative label to yourself after a negative experience	You spill your drink at a party and subsequently believe, "I am a clutz."
Dichotomous or polarized thinking/ all-or-none/ black-and-white	Categorizing things into one of two extremes	Believing that all lawyers are crooks and liars

Personalize	Attributing an event to yourself when there is actually little supporting evidence	A waiter is rude to you, and you believe that you did something to cause it when that person may simply not have felt well that day
Selective abstraction/ conclusion/isolated detail	Making a judgment based on limited information while ignoring other information	Focusing on the colleague who does not like you rather than focusing on the others who do like you

Forgiveness Therapy (FT)

A third cognitively-based therapy is Forgiveness Therapy (FT). Since the next chapter is solely dedicated to the investigation and explanation of biblical and secular forgiveness, this section will focus solely on an overview of forgiveness as a therapeutic modality. Forgiveness is not a biblical recommendation but a command from God since it affects all intrapersonal and interpersonal interactions. Understanding the reason for this command can help us be more accepting of forgiveness and more willing to practice forgiveness.

Forgiveness that is employed as a therapeutic modality is most effective when it focuses on the offended person rather than the offender. The offender will paradoxically benefit, which is explained in greater detail in the next chapter. It is difficult to ask a survivor of childhood sexual abuse to forgive the offender because it is good for that person! A wounded individual is unable to have compassion for the offender until the wound has healed.

The primary work in forgiveness therapy is to make a conscious, effortful choice of the will to release an offender from any debt owed. Forgiveness then begins as a cognitive act and requires a change in beliefs. One of the outcomes of forgiveness is to make a behavioral shift toward the offender. Another goal of forgiving is to stir up feelings of compassion toward the offender: empathy. This is a prime example of how affect, behavior, and cognitions interact with one another and greatly influence one another.

The following table compares and contrasts the therapies described in this chapter. It defines and delineates the issues related to the analysis of not only a theoretical model but also the modality as a treatment. It lists the basic components of treatment necessary for change and indicates which components are deemed important in each therapy.

	Forgiveness Therapy	Dialectical Behavior Therapy	Cognitive Behavior Therapy	Rational Emotive Behavior Therapy	Behavior Therapy
Awareness	Necessary for change	Necessary for change	Necessary for change	Necessary for change	Not necessary
Responsibility	On the self	On the self	On the self	On the self	Not necessary
Insight	Necessary for change	Necessary for change	Necessary for change	Necessary for change	Not necessary
Active/Directive	Both client and therapist	Both client and therapist	Both client and therapist	Both client and therapist	Both client and therapist
Behavior	Change action toward offender	Validation by therapist	Not addressed	Indirectly affected	Focal point emphasis
Thoughts	Primary to change	Validation by therapist	Self-understanding	Considered either rational or irrational	Not addressed
Emotions	Compassion for offender	Acceptance of self, others, and life	Indirectly affected	Attack shame	Not addressed

Summary of Scripture versus Forgiveness Therapy

Forgiveness therapy incorporates all the aspects of the behavior therapies as well as some treatment modalities which were not mentioned herein. This is indicative of the ability for a therapist to employ forgiveness therapy simultaneously with other modalities to achieve a successful outcome for the client. As far as forgiveness therapy versus scripture, it goes without saying that forgiveness definitely lines up with the Word of God as well as his purposes and plans for our lives. Yet, man cannot forgive on his own strength. Secular and Christian researchers have, for the most part, left God out of the practice of forgiving, which is unrealistic since he is the one who created forgiveness and first implemented it as a model for mankind. Forgiveness therapy works only when it is employed with the help of the Holy Spirit.

Summary of Scripture versus Cognitive Therapy

Reasonableness, understanding, honor, loveliness, and excellence bring our spirits up rather than dragging them down according to scripture. God charges us to make the choice to change our negative-thinking patterns into those which are positive. Secular research supports God's directive and give us detailed instructions for making the changes happen. CBT techniques include identifying cognitive distortions (negative beliefs), stopping cognitive distortions, challenging negative distortions, and replacing cognitive distortions. Cognitive therapy places responsibility on the client to take control of her/his thoughts rather than being controlled by external events.

Cognitive theories do not line up with the Word of God in that they purport man can always solve his own problems by changing his thoughts. Human beings are fallible, and followers of Christ are told to seek God's help when we are unable to successfully cope on our own. The Holy Spirit that comes to live inside us when we receive Christ guides us into all truth (John 16:13), empowers us (Luke 4:14), comforts us (Acts 9:31), and gives us wisdom (Luke 21:15).

Conclusion

God, who created mankind and gifted him with freewill, better understands us than we ourselves. Man's attempts to understand and change human nature cannot effectively do so without admitting to the sinful nature within each person. Man's attempts to build upon behavioral theories by first including thoughts and finally including feelings in his psychology still falls short of curing the intrapersonal and interpersonal problems individuals face. Albert Einstein (1939) has been attributed with the idea that "science without religion is lame and that religion without science is blind." Far too long the church has exhibited a derisive attitude toward psychology, and psychologists have snubbed Christianity. It is time for the two to be reconciled. God created doctors and scientists to benefit mankind and to serve a specific purpose.

The Bible contains all that we need to know to live abundant lives, but it does not give us the details of exactly how to incorporate all its benefits into reality. That pleasure has been left for us to seek out, discover, develop, and implement. God has created a mystery for us to uncover as life unfolds. He leads us along one step at a time allowing us to desire more of him and deeper answers to our life's questions. Psychotherapy is an important piece of the healing that we desire and that God the Father desires for us. All of its components are written in his holy word.

2

What Is Biblical Forgiveness?

A GREAT FALLACY about Christianity is that it is based on love. Rather, it is based upon forgiveness. Christianity is the only world religion that is solely based on forgiveness, which is born out of love. There are faithful Muslims, compassionate Buddhists, gentle and patient Hindus. Yet, the one true God of Israel is the only one who ultimately forgave and demands that we forgive others sacrificially with his divine help. Without forgiveness, there is no Christianity. God could have given us the fruit of the spirit (love, joy, peace, patience, kindness, goodness, faithfulness, gentleness, self-control), and it would have been *fruitless* because there was no loving forgiveness of sin or eternal life.

Jesus Christ can be seen throughout the entire Bible, hidden in the word pictures of the verses. In the Old

Testament (OT) the Hebrews prayed to God to forgive them, and the priests performed animal sacrifices on behalf of their sins. The shadow of Jesus Christ's atonement is in the original Hebrew language but, unfortunately, was omitted by medieval Bible translators. In the New Testament (NT), his life story was openly revealed through the writers by the Holy Spirit.

We have records of his death for our collective sake. He is our role model, and we forgive because God directs us to do so, not whether we feel like forgiving at the time. Our model for holy living continues to be Jesus Christ. God told us to be holy for he is holy (Lev. 11:44; 1 Pet. 1:16). We cannot be holy in and of ourselves because Adam and Eve sinned, and we were born with a sin nature (Josh. 24:19). We need Jesus Christ to perpetually forgive our sins, shortcomings, and mistakes. With help from God's Holy Spirit, we can be encouraged, empowered, and strengthened to forgive.

God's Supreme Authority and Power to Forgive

God's forgiveness toward men was a sign of his supreme headship. Forgiveness in the OT was a sign of power and authority. In ancient cultures, only earthly kings and rulers could forgive a grievous sin and had the final word over life and death. This is revealed to us in the NT book of Matthew (18:21–35), which tells the story of a wicked, unforgiving servant. The servant owed his master an astronomical sum of money that was so large it could never have been repaid. The scriptures tell us that only the master of the household was able to forgive the debt or decide to hold the servant accountable. The penalty would have been imprisonment until his death or his immediate death in the presence of the king. The master in this story is symbolically referring to God who is able to forgive our astronomical, insurmountable sin debts.

> And out of pity for him, the master of that servant released him and forgave him the debt. (Matt. 18:27)

> But with you there is forgiveness, that you may be feared. (Ps. 130:4)

> To the Lord our God belong mercy and forgiveness, for we have rebelled against Him. (Dan. 9:9)

> Help us, O God of our salvation, for the glory of your name; deliver us and forgive our sins for your name's sake. (Ps. 79:9)

> For your name's sake, O Lord, pardon my guilt, for it is great. (Ps. 25:11)

I am writing to you, little children, because your sins are forgiven for his name's sake. (1 John 2:12)

God's Forgiveness Is a Sign That We Belong to Him

Those who have received eternalness by believing in and following Jesus Christ are considered children of the Most High God (Ps. 82:6). We have been grafted into the vine of God (adopted) through Jesus Christ (Rom. 11:17). As children of God, we are benefactors of the blessings of our adoption, which is perpetual forgiveness of all our sins.

> For you did not receive the spirit of slavery to fall back into fear, but you have received the Spirit of adoption as sons, by whom we cry, "Abba! Father!" (Rom. 8:15)

> You forgave the iniquity of your people; you covered all their sin. (Ps. 85:2)

> Then hear from heaven your dwelling place and forgive and render to each whose heart you know, according to all his ways, for you, you only, know the hearts of the children of mankind. (1 Kings 8:39; 2 Chron. 6:30)

If my people who are called by my name humble themselves, and pray and seek my face and turn from their wicked ways, then I will hear from heaven and will forgive their sin and heal their land. (2 Chron. 7:14)

God's Forgiveness Is a Blood Covenant

Life is in the blood, which flows through living creatures. It carries our DNA and RNA. It carries necessary oxygen and nutrients to the entire body. It is a waste disposal system. When the blood is poisoned by disease or toxins, the entire body is sick. When the blood is healthy, the body can maintain health in every area.

God required blood sacrifice because life is in the blood. Sin is so deadly (either directly or indirectly) that it requires a death for its atonement. In the Old Testament, the blood of animals was used daily, weekly, seasonally, or yearly to atone for the sins of the people (Lev. 4:20, 26, 31, 35; 5:10, 13, 16, 18; 6:7; 19:22; Num. 15:25, 26, 28; Deut. 21:8). The temple must have looked like a slaughterhouse more than the house of God at times. The priests were trained as butchers as much as they were trained to worship God. The rituals for how to divide the animals and the organs were specific. The parts that were to be burned and offered to God versus the parts that could be eaten by the priests were also detailed in scripture.

Fortunately for us, when Jesus died on the cross, his death did away with the sacrifices of animals. His shed blood was sinless, and the blood of goats and bulls could not equal it (Heb. 10:4). We are spared not only from eternal damnation, but also from the need to continue killing innocent animals.

> Indeed, under the law almost everything is purified with blood, and without the shedding of blood there is no forgiveness of sins. (Heb. 9:22)

> For this is my blood of the covenant, which is poured out for many, for the forgiveness of sins. (Matt. 26:28)

> In Him we have redemption through His blood, the forgiveness of our trespasses, according to the riches of His grace. (Eph. 1:7)

God's Forgiveness Is Complete and Eternal

One cannot argue with the word of God. When he grants us eternal life, it is complete. All our sins are covered for eternity. He made a vital statement from the cross just before he died. All of Christianity hinges upon it, yet many religious people believe that we can lose our salvation once we have gained it as a free gift. "When Jesus had received the sour wine, he said, 'It is finished,' and he bowed his head and gave up his spirit" (John 19:30).

Nowhere in scripture does it state clearly that we can lose our salvation. If we could lose our salvation, God is faithful, and he would make it evidently plain. He would not use parables or hide it in quizzical stories. You can't even give your salvation back to God. You are sealed with his Holy Spirit.

> For I will forgive their iniquity, and I will remember their sin no more. (Jer. 31:34)

> You forgave the iniquity of your people; you covered *all* their sin. (Ps. 85:2; italics mine)

> You will cast *all* our sins into the depths of the sea. (Mic. 7:19; italics mine)

> I will remember their sins and lawless deeds no more. Where there is forgiveness of these, there is no longer any offering for sin. (Heb. 10:17–18)

Jesus's example of praying for forgiveness is given to us in what is known as the Lord's Prayer (Matt. 6:9–13). In those verses Jesus tells us to ask God to forgive us as we forgive others. We are eternally secure, but we are to consider our new daily sins and then ask for forgiveness. We also ask our heavenly father to help us avoid the temptation that can lead to sin since it is so devastating to us and others. Many people avoid thinking about their sins because, like Adam and Eve, they are ashamed of their actions and themselves. Like Adam and Eve, they feel the embarrassment of being naked before God, others, and themselves. When we don't seek God's forgiveness daily, it is because we are looking at ourselves and our behaviors through human eyes, not the eyes of our loving Father who wants to forgive us and already provided it for us. God enjoys being reminded that his son died in our place and was victorious over death.

Some religious leaders have used individual passages in scripture, which have either been taken out of context or do not refer to followers of Christ, to support their stance that our salvation is never secure until we die. The following is one example:

> Then the kingdom of heaven will be like ten virgins who took their lamps and went to meet the bridegroom. Five of them were foolish, and five were wise. For when the foolish took their lamps, they took no

oil with them, but the wise took flasks of oil with their lamps. As the bridegroom was delayed, they all became drowsy and slept. But at midnight there was a cry, "Here is the bridegroom! Come out to meet him." Then all those virgins rose and trimmed their lamps. And the foolish said to the wise, "Give us some of your oil, for our lamps are going out." But the wise answered, saying "Since there will not be enough for us and for you, go rather to the dealers and buy for yourselves." And while they were going to buy, the bridegroom came, and those who were ready went in with him to the marriage feast, and the door was shut. Afterward the other virgins came also, saying, "Lord, lord, open to us." But he answered, "Truly, I say to you, I do not know you." Watch therefore, for you know neither the day nor the hour. (Matt. 25:1–13)

This scripture has been used to illustrate the idea that some believers will not make it into heaven, that some will be caught short of the necessary spiritual awareness and thereby miss the Lord's coming. One fundamental error in this thinking is the erroneous focus. The Lord is not addressing all believers. His audience was not Gentiles who came to believe in Christ as the Messiah. He was addressing the disciples: Jewish believers. Romans 11:17 states that some branches from Abraham's tree (the Jews) were broken off the main vine while some wild shoots were grafted in (Gentiles) and now are part of the family of God. Those Jews who do not believe in Jesus as Messiah are broken off the vine, while Gentiles who believe in Jesus for the forgiveness of sins are grafted into the vine or adopted into the family of God (2 Cor. 6:18). They are the foolish virgins in the above passage that did not have enough oil to light their lamps and at the last moment ran out to buy some.

This leads to the symbolic meaning and importance of the oil. The oil referred to in Nehemiah, Hosea, Deuteronomy, and Joel is *yishtar*. *Yishtar* in the Hebrew language means "producing light and anointing." The Greek word for the oil referred to in Matthew 25 is *elaion*, which refers to olive oil. The oil is a representation of the Holy Spirit, which produces light (Strong's 2010). So the virgins who had oil represent those people who have been born again through Christ and, through Christ, are filled with the Holy Spirit (oil, light). The foolish virgins who took no oil with them represent people who have no relationship with Jesus Christ and do not have the Holy Spirit living in them. This indicates that these are not believers who have somehow lost their salvation but people who have never received eternal life through Jesus Christ. We can grieve the Holy Spirit or quench his work, but the scriptures do not state that we ever lose the Holy Spirit. The difference between the wise and foolish virgins is obvious. The wise virgins are those who already believe in Jesus Christ while the foolish virgins are people who do not.

Unforgiveness Is a Curse

How dare we curse others with unforgiveness when God so blesses us with forgiveness? We are rich beyond measure when we have been saved through faith in Christ Jesus. We have no right to cause others to carry the burden of unforgiveness when Jesus Christ bore our burden of sin on the cross. When we hold unforgiveness toward others, we actually end up carrying the burden of unforgiveness rather than laying it on their shoulders. The following scriptures indicates how uninformed and empty the unforgiving follower of Christ:

> And whenever you stand praying, forgive, if you have anything against anyone, so that your Father also who is in heaven may forgive you your trespasses. (Mark 11:25)

> Be kind to one another, tenderhearted, forgiving one another, as God in Christ forgave you. (Eph. 4:32)

Put on then, as God's chosen ones, holy and beloved, compassionate hearts, kindness, humility, meekness, and patience, bearing with one another and, if one has a complaint against another, forgiving each other; as the Lord has forgiven you, so you also must forgive. (Col. 3:12–13)

God Forgives Us because He Loves Us

It is a blessing and an honor to be forgiven when we sin. We should not be ashamed afterward that we needed his forgiveness. It is the most loving thing God can do for us. Without forgiveness, there is no salvation, no eternal life, and no reason to exist!

Yet he, being compassionate, atoned for their iniquity and did not destroy them; he restrained his anger often and did not stir up all his wrath. (Ps. 78:38)

Blessed is the one whose transgression is forgiven, whose sin is covered. (Ps. 32:1)

For you, O Lord, are good and forgiving, abounding in steadfast love to all who call upon you. (Ps. 86:5)

Blessed are those whose lawless deeds are forgiven, and whose sins are covered; blessed is the man against whom the Lord will not count his sin. (Rom. 4:7–8)

Who is a God like You, pardoning iniquity and forgiving transgression for the remnant of His inheritance? He does not retain His anger forever, because He delights in steadfast love [agape]. He will again have compassion on us; He will tread our iniquities underfoot. (Mic. 7:18–19)

We Are Assured of Forgiveness When We Confess Our Sins

It's better if we don't ignore or try to hide our sins. God sees them anyway. When we admit our sins to ourselves and confess them to him, he responds with forgiveness automatically. He even knows we will sin again, and he still forgives us and has already forgiven our future sins.

I acknowledged my sin to you, and I did not cover my iniquity; I said, 'I will confess my transgressions to the Lord,' and you forgave the iniquity of my sin. (Ps. 32:5)

If we say we have no sin we deceive ourselves and the truth is not in us. If we confess our sins, He is faithful and just to forgive us our sins and cleanse us from all unrighteousness. (1 John 1:8–9)

God Forgives Us Even When We Are Complicit in the Offense

God forgives the believer even when the injured person is complicit in her/his own injury or sin. For instance, in the OT, if a woman made foolish vows or pledges to the Lord, her father or husband could release her from them, and the Lord would forgive her (Num. 30:8, 12). Not only might we say regrettable things or make foolish promises, but we may respond in a negative manner when we allow someone else to hurt us. Even though another person may offend us, it is not appropriate to become part of the problem by sinning in response to the offense. We take responsibility for our actions whether we are the root of the problem or are just a branch.

Consider my affliction and trouble and forgive all my sins. (Ps. 25:18)

Therefore I tell you, her sins, which are many, are forgiven-for she loved much. But he who is forgiven little, loves little. (Luke 7:47)

Jesus Christ Is Our Role Model of Forgiveness

Jesus was our example when he was being crucified, and although we will never die for the sins of all mankind, we can symbolically be crucified with Christ. We use his example of forgiveness as template for our forgiveness. He forgives not only our actions but intentions of our hearts (Acts 8:22). Yet, God made us alive together with Christ in the Spirit, and our fleshly sins are dead (Col. 2:13).

> God exalted him at his right hand as Leader and Savior, to give repentance to Israel and forgiveness of sins. (Acts 5:31)

> Let it be known to you therefore, brothers, that through this man forgiveness of sins is proclaimed to you, and by him everyone who believes is freed from everything from which you could not be freed by the law of Moses. (Acts 13:38–39)

> To open their eyes, so that they may turn from darkness to light and from the power of Satan to God, that they may receive forgiveness of sins and a place among those who are sanctified by faith in me. (Acts 26:18)

In him we have redemption through his blood, the forgiveness of our trespasses, according to the riches of his grace. (Eph. 1:7)

In whom we have redemption the forgiveness of sins. (Col. 1:14)

And Jesus said, "Father, forgive them, for they know not what they do." (Luke 23:34)

Be kind to one another, tenderhearted, forgiving one another, as God in Christ forgave you. (Eph. 4:32)

[B]earing with one another and, if one has a complaint against another, forgiving each other; as the Lord has forgiven you, so you also must forgive. (Col. 3:13)

We Are Commanded to Forgive Others

Although we may struggle with unforgiveness, we are commanded to participate in the death of Christ by granting mercy to others in a form of communion, which reminds God of his son's sacrifice. It would be unjust for him to forgive us all our sins but allow us to continue holding unforgiveness against anyone else and thus create a world of bitterness and hatred. Jesus's sacrifice covered all our sins for a lifetime. Then, can we not forgive others when they continue to sin against us?

> And forgive us our debts as we forgive our debtors. (Matt. 6:12; Luke 11:4)

> For if you forgive others their trespasses, your heavenly Father will also forgive you, but if you do not forgive others their trespasses, neither will your Father forgive your trespasses. (Matt. 6:14–15)

> Then Peter came up and said to him, "Lord, how often will my brother sin against me, and I forgive him? As many as seven times?" Jesus said to him, "I do not say to you seven times, but seventy-seven times." (Matt. 18:21–22)

> And whenever you stand praying, forgive, if you have anything against anyone, so that your Father also who is in heaven may forgive you your trespasses. (Mark 11:25–26)

> Judge not, and you will not be judged; condemn not, and you will not be condemned; forgive, and you will be forgiven. (Luke 6:37; 7:47–48)

Anyone whom you forgive, I also forgive. Indeed, what I have forgiven, if I have forgiven anything, has been for your sake in the presence of Christ. (2 Cor. 2:10)

We are particularly obligated to forgive someone when they apologize. We are not to analyze whether or not the contrition is genuine. We are simply to set a good example by forgiving without arguing.

Pay attention to yourselves! If your brother sins, rebuke him, and if he repents, forgive him, and if he sins against you seven times in the day, and turns to you seven times, saying, "I repent," you must forgive him. (Luke 17:3–4)

So you should rather turn to forgive and comfort him, or he may be overwhelmed by excessive sorrow. (2 Cor. 2:7)

Forgiving Family Members

Examples of family members forgiving one another in scripture are frequent. Scriptures tell us how family members are to treat one another and where boundary lines are drawn. "But if anyone does not provide for his relatives, and especially for members of his household, he has denied the faith and is worse than an unbeliever" (1 Tim. 5:8).

Jacob was betrayed by his uncle, Laban (Gen. 30–31); Jacob betrayed his jealous brother, Esau, by stealing his birthright (Gen. 25–27); Joseph was betrayed by all of his jealous brothers and sold into slavery (Gen. 50:17); Absalom betrayed his half-brother, Amnon, to avenge the rape of his sister (2 Sam. 13); Absalom betrayed his father, King David, trying to take over the throne (2 Sam. 15); Jeremiah was betrayed by his family and his entire nation (Jer. 12). Relationships and forgiveness are specifically addressed as God knows how difficult it is to forgive those closest to us. For most people, betrayal by a loved one is more difficult to bear or to repair the relationship.

> Husbands, love your wives, as Christ loved the church and gave himself up for her. (Eph. 5:25)

> Husbands, love your wives, and do not be harsh with them. (Col. 3:19)

> Likewise, husbands, live with your wives in an understanding way, showing honor to the woman as the weaker vessel, since they are heirs with you of the grace of life, so that your prayers may not be hindered. (1 Pet. 3:7)

And so train the young women to love their husbands and children, to be self-controlled, pure, working at home, kind, and submissive to their own husbands, that the word of God may not be reviled. (Titus 2:4–5)

Fathers, do not provoke your children to anger, but bring them up in the discipline and instruction of the Lord. (Eph. 6:4)

Children, obey your parents in the Lord, for this is right. "Honor your father and mother" (this is the first commandment with a promise), "that it may go well with you and that you may live long in the land." (Eph. 6:1–3)

Keeping steadfast love for thousands, forgiving iniquity and transgression and sin, but who will by no means clear the guilty, visiting the iniquity of the fathers on the children and the children's children, to the third and the fourth generation. (Exod. 34:7; Num. 14:18)

We Are Commanded to Forgive Our Enemies

When the prophet Jeremiah, in chapter 12 of his book, prayed against his enemies, God's answer was that all the people (godly and ungodly alike) should be warned of the approaching disaster. Even though God was going to visit the disaster on them on account of their sins, he also wanted them to have the opportunity to repent.

God requires that we forgive our enemies, which differentiates us from unbelievers. It is easy to forgive someone who loves us, but forgiving someone who hates us or repeatedly hurts us is most challenging.

> But I say to you, "Love your enemies and pray for those who persecute you". (Matt. 5:44)

> Repay no one evil for evil, but give thought to do what is honorable in the sight of all. If possible, so far as it depends on you, live peaceably with all. Beloved, never avenge yourselves, but leave it to the wrath of God, for it is written, "Vengeance is mine, I will repay, says the Lord." To the contrary, "if your enemy is hungry, feed him; if he is thirsty, give him something to drink; for by so doing you will heap burning coals on his head." Do not be overcome by evil, but overcome evil with good. (Rom. 12:17–21)

Believers Pray for Forgiveness on Behalf of Other Believers

Believers petitioned God on behalf of the sins of other believers in scripture. Moses begged God not to destroy his children who were involved in the formation and worship of the golden calf while he was on Mt. Sinai receiving the Ten Commandments (Exod. 32:32). Again, Moses interceded on behalf of the Hebrews in the desert when they rebelled against his authority. "Please pardon the iniquity of this people, according to the greatness of your steadfast love, just as you have forgiven this people, from Egypt until now" (Num. 14:19).

King Solomon, during his prayer of dedication for the temple he had built for God's people, asked God to hear not only his prayers but the prayers of all Israel (1 Kings 8:30; 2 Chron. 6:21, 39). He reminded God that they were his people and that his desire was to forgive them. He also asked God to forgive Israel in the future when the people would sin and turn away from him (1 Kings 8:34; 2 Chron. 6:25). Further, he requested that when God would forgive his people, he would bless them as well (1

Kings 8:36; 2 Chron. 6:27). Finally, he prayed that they would have favor with their enemies (1 Kings 8:50).

Daniel (9:19) prayed on behalf of Jerusalem according to the writings of Jeremiah. It was seventy years after the desolation of Jerusalem. Amos (7:2) had a vision of locusts devastating Israel. His response was to ask God to forgive the people and rescue them from the impending disaster. God's response to Amos's petition was to relent concerning the matter and forgive the nation (Amos 7:3).

Believers Pray for Forgiveness on Behalf of Unbelievers

Pharaoh, who did not believe in the God of the Hebrews, asked that Moses petition God on behalf of the Egyptian people (Exod. 10:17). In that situation, the heathen people witnessed how powerful the God of the universe was firsthand. The most powerful story of a believer praying for an unbeliever is when Jesus Christ prayed for the thief who was crucified with him (Luke 23:39–43).

We Receive the Holy Spirit When We Are Initially Forgiven for Our Sins

"And Peter said, 'Repent and be baptized every one of you in the name of Jesus Christ for the forgiveness of your sins, and you will receive the gift of the Holy Spirit.'" (Acts 2:38)

Forgiveness and Healing Are Intricately Connected

Our emotional, physical, and psychological healing is intricately connected to the forgiveness we extend to others. Unforgiveness itself is seen as a sin by God. Although our healing is connected to our forgiveness of others, there are also examples of our healing being connected to our own forgiveness.

> And should not you have had mercy on your fellow servant, as I had mercy on you? And in anger his master delivered him to the jailers, until he should pay all his debt. So also my heavenly Father will do to every one of you, if you do not forgive your brother from your heart. (Matt. 18:33–35)

> See to it that no one fails to obtain the grace of God; that no "root of bitterness" springs up and

causes trouble, and by it many become defiled. (Heb. 12:15)

For I see that you are in the gall of bitterness and in the bond of iniquity. (Acts 8:23)

And no inhabitant will say, "I am sick" the people who dwell there will be forgiven their iniquity. (Isa. 33:24)

Who forgives all your iniquity, who heals all your diseases. (Ps. 103:3)

Jesus forgave sins during his earthly ministry so that people could obtain all forms of healing. Most of the examples pertain to physical healing.

But that you may know that the Son of Man has authority on earth to forgive sins, he then said to the paralytic. "Rise, pick up your bed and go home." (Matt. 9:2, 5–6; Mark 2:5, 9–10; Luke 5:20, 23)

And the prayer of faith will save the one who is sick, and the Lord will raise him up. And if he has committed sins, he will be forgiven. (James 5:15)

We Apologize to One Another and Seek Forgiveness

This is an area that is basically silent in the church but not in scripture. We are told to forgive, but we rarely hear that people should, of their own volition, seek forgiveness not only from God but from those who they have offended. Often Christians refuse to take responsibility for their actions.

> Therefore, confess your sins to one another and pray for one another, that you may be healed. The prayer of a righteous person has great power as it is working. (James 5:16)

> So if you are offering your gift at the altar and there remember that your brother has something against you, leave your gift there before the altar and go. First be reconciled to your brother, and then come and offer your gift. (Matt. 5:23–24)

We might even seek forgiveness on behalf of an offender to the offended party. An example of this is in 1 Samuel 25:28. Abigail entreated King David to forgive her foolish, abusive husband for insulting him. It worked to her benefit because her husband died suddenly, and she became King David's wife!

When Might We Not Be Forgiven?

It is important to clearly state that there is only one sin for which anyone will spend eternity separated from God, and that is to reject Jesus Christ's sacrifice of forgiveness. We don't go to hell for committing acts that are opposed to God's laws but for not receiving the free gift of forgiveness, which came through the death of Christ.

> Therefore I tell you, every sin and blasphemy will be forgiven people, but the blasphemy against the Spirit will not be forgiven. And whoever speaks a word against the Son of Man will be forgiven, but whoever speaks against the Holy Spirit will not be forgiven, either in this age or in the age to come. (Matt. 12:31–32)

3

What Is Secular Forgiveness?

Aristotle and Virtues

IT WAS ARISTOTLE'S belief that to know anything, we must ask questions (trans. 1985). Once questions have been posed, researchers create hypotheses that guide them in the direction of possibly answering those questions. What is forgiveness? Forgiveness research began with a philosophical construct that forgiveness is a virtue. A virtue, by definition, has the quality of being good in and of itself (Woolf 1980). That means forgiveness is, by nature, inherently good. In *Nicomachean Ethics*, Aristotle (trans. 1985) wrote about virtues as teleological entities performed by character-driven people. People do not just talk about what is good but become good by practicing virtues. Later, this led Simon (1986) to write that an understanding of philosophy is the beginning of the understanding of the definition of forgiveness. Aristotle defined virtues by identifying seven characteristics they have in common.

First, a virtue is performed for the benefit of all mankind (Aristotle 1926). Second, the one performing the virtue is motivated to do something good. Third, the person performing the virtue is consciously aware that s/he is doing something good (Aristotle 1925). Fourth, a virtue develops and deepens with practice. Fifth, the expression of the virtue need not be perfect, but it becomes more perfect with practice (Aristotle 1955). Sixth, each person will differ uniquely in their expression of the virtue. Seventh, the practice of virtue requires consistency (Aristotle 1980).

The problem with philosophy is that, by definition, it is "the love of wisdom" (Woolf 1980). Wisdom does not equate to practical reality. There must be a motivational force between wisdom and action. Having wisdom or knowledge about forgiveness does not mean that people will actually practice forgiving. The material in this text will show the path that leads from the point of understanding forgiveness to the point of practicing forgiveness. Yet, without the foundational wisdom, forgiveness would be a vague concept to which most individuals would be oblivious. From the foundation of wisdom arose research the goal of which was to discover the exact nature of forgiveness. As stated in the first line of this text, Aristotle believed that to know anything, one must ask questions. Researchers began to ask specific questions about how individuals forgive, and those research questions created an open door for practical knowledge to emerge (Noll 2005; Orathinkal and Vansteenwegen 2006; Witvliet 2005; Witvliet, Ludwig, and VanderLann 2001; Witvliet, Phipps, Feldman, and Beckham 2004; Worthington, Jr. 2001, 2005).

Research subjects, who were recruited into the studies, had experienced traumas and offenses ranging from military combat, to incest, to rape, to domestic violence, to relationship betrayal. Quantitative and qualitative data were collected and analyzed. It indicated that underneath the practical and accepted knowledge about forgiveness were myths about forgiveness, and underlying both of those issues was the basic human fear of forgiving.

Fears about Forgiving

As stated in chapter one of this text, human beings operate through actions, thoughts, and emotions. Although fear is an emotion, it is the expression of the belief system of the injured person. Emotions are powerful. Fear is probably the most powerful emotion since it is the foundation for anger, aversion, cruelty, embarrassment, guilt, hatred, shame, and sorrow. Emotions can completely overtake some individuals in such a way that they cannot function, particularly after an offense. Fear that is experienced after an offense can block healing. It is common for offended individuals to wonder why God or a higher power would allow something painful to happen to them.

The researchers cited above found that people were afraid of (1) anger with God, (2) anger with the offender who may also have been.... a loved one, (3) anger with one's self, (4) opening oneself up to being hurt again, (5) continued dislike of the offender, (6) pretending nothing happened, (7) inability to forgive, (8) taking no action, (9) letting the offender get away with an offense, and (10) keeping the offense a secret.

Often an offended person will attempt to deny anger toward God or a higher power because it is considered taboo. Unfortunately, that only makes matters worse. If the offender was a close family member, a loved one, or a friend, the offended person may also experience difficulty admitting experiencing angry emotions. It is socially unacceptable in some cultures to express anger toward a parent, a spouse, or a lifelong friend. So, here again, the offended person may try to hide the anger and unforgiveness, which only festers internally. Finally, anger toward one's self is not uncommon even when the offended person was not complicit in the offense. Unfortunately, children and adolescents often take responsibility for the inappropriate actions of adults who have neglected or abused them.

It is understandable that the injured person would fear being hurt again when the injury or betrayal that was inflicted was deep or repetitive. It is also interesting to note that many injured people are afraid they cannot forgive because their feelings toward the offender will never change. That is actually an encouraging indication of a general desire, among those who were studied, to want to forgive. The injured person may also believe that s/he must like the offender to have truly forgiven. When we forgive, we forgive the person, not the behavior. Their behavior is still wrong or hurtful. When a client tells me that s/he doesn't like the offender, it can generally be discovered that the injured person doesn't like what the person did, but can still like or love the person.

For example, a former client's husband was viewing pornography on the Internet. That was a deep betrayal for her. She continued to be incapable of trusting him, but she still loved him. Her confusion was that she couldn't separate his behavior from who he was or his identity. I worked to help her forgive him while still knowing that the act of viewing pornography was wrong. In the end, she continued to struggle with really wanting to forgive him (he did apologize) and not wanting to forgive him (she could never trust him again).

After the initial intense emotional response occurs due to an offense, our beliefs and thoughts emerge. Faulty thinking about forgiveness includes having to keep the offense secret, having to pretend that nothing happened, continued disgust with or dislike of the offender, and that forgiveness is unachievable. It must be noted that these concepts can be part of reality and not just an individual response. Society as well as influential members in the person's life may counsel the injured person to keep what happened a secret, or to stop thinking about the injury. The reasons vary, but basically, most people don't have healthy coping skills themselves and don't know how to help someone else who is hurting. These faulty thinking processes then lead to faulty behavior. (I use the term *faulty* not to degrade anyone but to indicate that they are not helpful for the injured person).

Then there are the behavioral components of forgiving, which include not being able to take action about the offense, letting someone get away with the offense (again, not taking action), keeping what happened a secret (again, not taking action).

Myths about Forgiving

The preceding common fears about forgiveness led researchers to uncover the following common myths about forgiveness. They include some of the following. Forgiveness is (1) for the weak; (2) forgetting; (3) hiding the feelings about the offense; (4) pardoning, condoning, or excusing; (5) reconciliation; (6) trusting the offender again; (7) the same concept as feeling less unforgiving toward an offender; (8) an acceptable form of smug self-righteousness; (9) keeping score of offenses; and (10) an excuse to look for offenses where there are none.

While there may be a grain of truth couched within those myths, they are inaccurate. An accurate understanding of forgiveness can be distorted by cognitive errors passed from generation to generation. To better understand the formulation of the definition of forgiveness, it is best to understand the current accepted secular knowledge about this virtue.

Accepted Forgiveness Knowledge

The first important fact about forgiveness is that forgiveness is difficult. Forgiveness requires taking mental action that will change our patterns of thinking. If forgiveness was easy, everyone would automatically do it. This is the most important point about forgiveness therapy, particularly for psychotherapy practitioners. It is a grave mistake to try to force someone to forgive. It is also a mistake to try to block someone from forgiving an offender. An effective psychotherapist will not only facilitate healthy growth for the individual, but will understand the timing of forgiveness. Each person forgives as s/he is ready to do so.

Second, forgiveness is an active choice requiring effortful psychological employment. Therefore, forgiveness is on a continuum. There are degrees of forgiveness from slight to complete. Forgiveness is only a philosophic concept until it is put into practice. The more you practice it, the better you become at forgiving. Otherwise, it does no good for the injured person, the offender, or society. The employment of forgiveness, like any emotional and psychological process, takes time and practice. It can be compared to the grieving process. In fact, an element of forgiveness is grieving.

Third, forgiveness requires admitting that there has been an offense. Those individuals who are unaware of the offense, through either conscious efforts to bury it or unconscious awareness of the hurt and pain, will suffer emotional and physical consequences related to the unresolved issue. It is now common knowledge in the medical world that stress is the cause of most illnesses (Uchino et al. 2007). Unforgiveness or unresolved hurt is a large part of that stress.

Fourth, forgiveness requires that the injured person admit there are wounded feelings accompanying the offense. Each society, race, and culture has different rules for dealing with offenses. Some cultures require all individuals to hide their true emotions whether they positive or negative. It is also more common for men to hold in emotions that are considered weak, such as sadness or hurt. As stated previously, the unaddressed injury festers and leads to many types of emotional and physical problems.

Fifth, the injured person acknowledges that those feelings are natural and that the person has a right to experience those emotions for a period of time is essential. If the individual does not claim the right to feel injured and to admit that something is owed to her/him, the injury goes unresolved. The individual may continue in the belief that s/he was complicit in the injury and therefore must bear all the responsibility for the injury. It is important, before being able to mercifully release the offender, to know that something was owed to the injured person. Or else, what is there to release? Forgiveness is no longer a sacrifice or a gift. This will also be an important concept in the biblical view of forgiveness.

Sixth, once the individual consciously admits that an offense has been committed, s/he freely and consciously gives up the right to expect or receive the obligation owed by the offender. The word *forgive* contains the word *give*. It can be viewed as an act of mercy through the giving of a gift. This is not necessarily something that happens immediately and requires time. Variably, this also may be the lengthiest part of the forgiveness work for some individuals.

Seventh, forgiveness is for the injured person, although the offender benefits as well. Forgiveness also means extending to the offender the same gift we hope to receive when we offend others. If we hope to be forgiven when we offend someone else, it is only fair that we apply the golden rule: "Do unto others as you would have them do unto you." Forgiveness means going beyond oneself and one's own healing by finding understanding of the offender: history, lifestyle, motives.

Eighth, forgiveness is not based upon an apology. Control of the situation lies with the injured person, not the offender. Forgiveness cuts the chains between the survivor and the offender, removing the power the offender had over the injured person. Apologizing is not the norm. If the injured person waits for that before releasing the burden of the injury, it will be carried for a very long time. Forgiveness is a journey to freedom and empowerment.

Ninth, forgiveness is not justice. They are separate entities. You can forgive an offender and still seek justice. It is important for some individuals to remember not only the offender but the incident as well. Individuals of violent or repetitive harm must protect themselves by remaining separated from continued abuse. Forgiveness is very powerful, but it does not necessarily change the offender's behavior. You can forgive someone and still set boundaries and disagree with their behavior.

Tenth, spiritually-minded individuals find it easier to have compassion and forgive (Witvliet 2004). To understand the reasons behind that, we must look at the components of religious beliefs and practices. What then does God's Word say about forgiveness? How is it different from, or similar to, the secular research findings? You may be surprised that God's point of view can be substantiated in the natural, secular realm.

4

Why Forgive?

Biblical Reasons

THE GREAT CHRISTIAN revivals around the world have taken place when people repented and asked God for forgiveness. They repented for their personal sins, and they repented for the sins of a city, region, or nation. God loves repentance. He loves to be reminded of his gracious gift of forgiveness toward mankind through the death of his son on the cross. We, who cannot live holy and perfect lives or make atonement for our mistakes and sins, have been given provision through the blood of Jesus Christ. God urges us to forgive so that he will be free and unhindered to forgive us. He wants us to forgive so that we can live free from burdens and hindrances.

Forgiveness is also closely connected to emotional and physical healing as demonstrated in the scriptures in the previous chapter. When we forgive others, we are healed. We give God the job of seeking justice for us, and we are free to move on with our lives. The only exception is in cases in which the person has a legal right to seek earthly justice. Yet that individual is still commanded in scripture to forgive since forgiveness and justice are separate entities: meaning that you can forgive an offender and still take legal action on the offense. In fact, it may be even more important for that individual to forgive so that s/he can find the release and freedom from the more grievous offense; the greater the offense, the greater the gift of freedom. That works both ways. When we require forgiveness, we want it to be free and unreserved, particularly when our offense is grievous.

When we are able to receive forgiveness, we are healed emotionally and physically. Think about a time in your life when you offended someone (intentionally or unintentionally). Didn't it feel uncomfortable to see them? Even if you believed the situation was not your fault. When you admitted to yourself that you were part of the offense or wholly responsible for it, didn't it feel good to be forgiven? Didn't you feel relieved? The next time you saw that individual, you were able to interact with her/him in a different way—once the matter was cleared up. On the other hand, think about a time when you hurt someone, and that person would not forgive you. It was probably very uncomfortable to see her/him or spend time with her/him, regardless of whether or not the other individual treated you poorly in return. When we don't forgive our offenders that is how they feel toward us: uncomfortable. If the individual has no grounds for feeling offended by you, or you have apologized and/or made restitution for an offense but the individual will not or cannot forgive you, then it is out of your hands. They will reap the consequences of their own unforgiveness.

Unforgiveness is a heavy, cumbersome burden that steals our time and energy. I tell my clients that when you don't forgive, you are apt to ruminate on the injury. Rumination is what cows do when they eat. They chew, regurgitate their food, chew it some more, and regurgitate it again. This cycle repeats until that last bit of food has been pulverized. Every time you think about the person or the injury, you will rehearse the incident, which brings painful emotions. Unforgiveness means that you are renting valuable space in your head to someone who does not deserve it. It's like owning a beautiful, clean apartment that you rent to someone who punches holes in the walls, pulls out the plumbing, rips up the carpet or flooring, breaks the windows, etc., while you're living on the streets. It's better to keep the beautiful apartment and live in it yourself. God deserves our thoughts, time, and energy.

Finally, brothers, whatever is true, whatever is honorable, whatever is just, whatever is pure, whatever is lovely, whatever is commendable, if there is any excellence, if there is anything worthy of praise, think about these things. (Phil. 4:8)

Forgive As You Have Been Forgiven

Our unforgiveness can block God's work in our lives. It is not that God intends to punish us or withhold blessings from us, but a holy God cannot tolerate sin. When we come to eternal life through Jesus Christ, we still are subject to the processes that God set in motion. In his word, it states that he will not forgive us if we don't forgive others (Matt. 6:15). God does not allow us to live a double standard in which he forgives us, but we can hold onto our unforgiveness.

In Matthew chapter 18, Jesus explained to his disciples that the kingdom of heaven is like a certain king who wanted to reconcile accounts with his servants. One of the servants owed the master a fortune. The servant begged and pleaded with the master to give him more time to pay what he could never repay. The master was so moved that he forgave the debt altogether! He also allowed the servant to remain employed in his household.

One the other hand, a fellow servant owed the first servant a very small amount of money. The first servant grabbed his fellow servant by the throat and demanded that he repay immediately. His fellow servant fell at his feet begging for more time to repay. The first servant ordered his fellow servant sent to prison instead. The other servants were deeply upset by the injustice and told their master. When their master heard about it, he delivered him to be tortured until he could pay all that he owed, which was never.

In that story, God gave us a picture of the difference between his son's sacrifice for us, and the little that others owe us. It is selfish and arrogant for us to hold unforgiveness toward others for offending us. God gave so much more than we could imagine and set an example of how we are to live. To ignore that is an insult to Jesus' payment of our debts.

"He who conceals his sins does not prosper, but whoever confesses and renounces them finds mercy" (Proverbs 28:13). Yet, when we confess our sins, he is faithful and just to forgive our sins and cleanse us from all unrighteousness (1 John 1:9).

Empirical Evidence

The benefits of forgiveness have historic roots in religious and spiritual belief systems and practices. A broader picture has emerged that forgiveness may be important not just as a religious and spiritual practice but as a component of a comprehensive vision of health. The benefits are identified in the specific studies following.

5

What Are the Benefits
of Forgiving?

THE FOLLOWING BENEFITS are derived from the scriptures as well as from secular empirical evidence and are divided into sections that pertain to each. They apply to all mankind but have a greater effect in the lives of those who are spiritually-minded. I want to highlight and clarify that statement. When our lifestyles employ God's principles for living, we derive certain benefits. Even unbelievers will benefit when they practice God's formulas for living; although they may do so unintentionally. For instance, when you plant seeds of blessing by helping others, you will eventually reap the benefits of helping others so that you begin receiving help in return. Acts of helping are part of God's universal laws (I am not referring to the Ten Commandments in this instance but to the teachings throughout scriptures). The secular world would express it as, "What goes around, comes around." That is correct most of the time. Although there are people who help others and still seem to have bad luck, are accident prone, are poor, etc. Those instances are few and far between.

If all mankind, believers and unbelievers, benefit from God's laws, is there a greater benefit to having a relationship with God, Jesus Christ, and the Holy Spirit? Yes! For those of us who seek God's face and intentionally practice his principles for living, there is abundance. Without God, you may or may not benefit from helping others, but God promises that his children are always blessed. It may take time for the seeds we plant to sprout and grow, but we have the greater blessing of abundance in him.

Those believers who are not blessed in life probably have faulty belief systems since God wants to actively bless his children. They might believe that poverty is godly. They might believe that false humility is appropriate and that they should not expect anything in return for helping others. All of those negative or neutral beliefs are incorrect beliefs and are directly in opposition to what God has for his children.

Scriptural Benefits of Forgiving

Being Under God's Authority

God demonstrates his authority to mankind in that he created us by speaking everything into being (Gen. 1:3, 6, 8, 9, 11, 14, 20, 24, and 26). We would not fear or be in awe of a god who did not have authority over us. "But with you there is forgiveness that you may be feared" (Ps. 130:4). Jesus also spoke with authority and, through his words, performed creative miracles. When he was teaching the disciples and the people, he spoke as one having authority and not as their scribes (Matt. 7:29). After Jesus had cleansed the temple of money changers and cursed the fig tree, the chief priests and elders of the people asked him by what authority he was performing miracles (Matt. 21:23). Even they could see that he was operating from a higher level than they were and were jealous. So the safest place in the world to be is in the palm of God's hand where he is in control, and he never forgets you nor lets go of you. He is omnipotent or all-powerful. It is he who loves us with an eternal, burning love. Since God is the supreme authority in the universe, and all other gods are false gods, don't you want to be under his authority?

Behold, I have engraved you on the palms of my hands; your walls are continually before me. (Isa. 49:16)

All that the Father gives me will come to me, and whoever comes to me I will never cast out. (John 6:37)

Belonging to God

When we belong to God, we are sealed as his forever.

And it is God who establishes us with you in Christ, and has anointed us, and who has also put his seal on us and given us his Spirit in our hearts as a guarantee. (2 Cor. 1:21–22)

I give them eternal life, and they will never perish, and no one will snatch them out of my hand. (John 10:28)

If my people who are called by my name humble themselves, and pray and seek my face and turn from their wicked ways, then I will hear from heaven and will forgive their sin and heal their land. (2 Chron. 7:14)

The Hebrew word for "called by my name" is *qara* (kaw-raw´), which means to name an individual by a primary characteristic (Strong 2010). Qara indicates that the person will have a personality trait that identifies her/him with the meaning of the name. For instance, the name Jacob means "to supplant." The name Eve means "mother of all creation." So we are named by God's primary characteristics. We are identified as belonging to God when there is evidence of him in our lives through what he does for us by sanctifying, protecting, providing, healing, and shepherding us. The evidence that we belong to him is apparent when we seek, praise, worship, and serve him. We open the doors for his benefits to enter our lives. We forsake all other gods to serve him alone. We attempt to treat others just as well as he treats us. The more we practice loving him and others, the better we become at it.

Being Blessed by God

Who wouldn't want to be blessed by God? We are to desire God's blessings, to seek them out, and to remove all that blocks us from receiving them (i.e., unforgiveness).

The Hebrew word for blessing is *barak* (baw-rawk'). It literally means to kneel and bless God, and in so doing, man benefits as well. God blessed Adam and Eve by giving them permission to be fruitful. Noah was blessed with sons. God promised to bless Abraham, and those who bless the descendants of Abraham are blessed as well. We are to seek the blessing that was initiated with God. "Blessed is the one whose transgression is forgiven, whose sin is covered" (Ps. 32:1).

Being Forgiven by the Blood of Christ

Jesus Christ was beaten so badly that his blood poured out from his body long before he was nailed to the cross. Depictions of his death in the media cannot come close to the pain he suffered on our behalf. His blood was the atonement for our sin debt that we celebrate symbolically when we take communion.

> For this is my blood of the covenant which is poured out for the many for the forgiveness of sins. (Matt. 26:28)

> And forgive us our debts as we forgive our debtors. (Matt. 6:12; Luke 11:4)

We understand from scripture that the entire prayer the Lord taught us to pray hinges on forgiveness. Without forgiveness from God, we have no reason to exist since we would spend eternity separated from God. Without forgiving others, we cannot be blessed with forgiveness.

Learning to Be Like Christ
(Love, Humility, and Compassion)

> If then you have been raised with Christ, seek the
> things that are above, where Christ is, seated at the
> right hand of God. Set your minds on things that
> are above, not on things that are on earth. For you
> have died, and your life is hidden with Christ in
> God. When Christ who is your life appears, then
> you also will appear with him in glory. (Col. 3:1–4)

Although we do not automatically reach perfection when
we accept forgiveness for our sins, we are instructed to seek
holiness and to become like Jesus Christ. We know that it
is possible to grow and mature in that direction since the
Bible tells us that it is as though we have died and been
raised with Christ into heaven without even suffering the
torture he went through. There is no way you or I could
humble ourselves and die for the sins of all humanity, but
it is as though we have since we now belong to him. That is
something that is hard to fathom.

> Let each of you look not only to his own interests,
> but also to the interests of others. Have this mind
> among yourselves, which is yours in Christ Jesus,
> who, though he was in the form of God, did not

count equality with God a thing to be grasped, but
made himself nothing, taking the form of a servant,
being born in the likeness of men. (Phil. 2:1–7)

There is a growing narcissism and arrogance that blocks
many people who call themselves followers of Christ from
humbly serving others, which requires empathy. To be like
him is to study his life and know his character and characteristics, including the compassion he had. When we humble ourselves, he is faithful to lift us up.

Peace and Rest

The word for peace in the Greek language of the New
Testament is *eirene* (i-ray´-nay). It means to have prosperity and quietness. Westerners may not know that to wish
someone peace, at Christmas for instance, means that you
want them to have a life that is whole and complete. Peace in
Hebrew is *shalom*, which means more than peace. It means
welfare, prosperity, wealth, favor, rest, safety, completeness,
and wholeness. Forgiveness opens the door to shalom.

When we forgive others, we are telling God that we
trust him to deal with the injustice rather than carrying
that burden around with us all the time. Jehovah Mishpat
is the Lord who brings justice, and Jehovah Shalom is the
Lord who brings completeness and peace. When he brings

justice, it all works out for the best. That may also include beneficial justice for the offender as well. Forgiveness may turn a life around. When we rest and let him do the work, we have the completeness and wholeness of shalom. The only thing God tells us to fear in scripture is missing out on the promise of entering his rest. The following text explains the curse of missing God's rest:

> For who were those who heard and yet rebelled? Was it not all those who left Egypt led by Moses? And with whom was he provoked for forty years? Was it not with those who sinned, whose bodies fell in the wilderness? And to whom did he swear that they would not enter his rest, but to those who were disobedient? So, we see that they were unable to enter because of *unbelief.* Therefore, while the promise of entering his rest still stands, let us fear lest any of you should seem to have failed to reach it. For good news came to us just as to them, but the message they heard did not benefit them, because they were not united by faith with those who listened. For we who have believed enter that rest, as he has said, "As I swore in my wrath, 'They shall not enter my rest,'" although his works were finished from the foundation of the world. For he has somewhere spoken of the seventh day in this way: "And God rested on

the seventh day from all his works." And again in this passage he said, "They shall not enter my rest." Since therefore it remains for some to enter in, and those who formerly received the good news failed to enter because of disobedience, again he appoints a certain day, "Today," saying, through David so long afterward, in the words already quoted, "Today, if you hear his voice, do not harden your hearts." For if Joshua had given them rest God would not have spoken of another day later on. So then, there remains a Sabbath rest for the people of God, for whoever has entered God's rest has also rested from his works as God did from his. Let us therefore strive to enter that rest, so that no one may fall by the same sort of disobedience. (Heb. 3:16–4:11)

The writer of the epistle to the Hebrews points out that the Hebrews who came out of Egypt rebelled and were not allowed entrance to God's rest in the Promised Land. Their descendants, who were born during the forty-year sojourn, were allowed to enter the rest. The author warns us to not wander in a desert, missing God's rest because of our rebellion. The author then mentions the seventh day on which God rested. God gives us an example of rest. Rest is a good thing. He took one day off at the end of creation, and whoever has entered God's rest will also rest from his work as

God did from his. Forgiveness means that we rest and let God bring justice to the offensive situation.

Health

Jehovah Rapha is the Lord who heals or thoroughly makes whole. "Who forgives all your iniquity, who heals all your diseases" (Ps. 103:3).

Supernaturally, he is able to release healing to us when we forgive. He waits for faith and permission to work on our behalf. When we release a burden and allow God to handle the offense for us, our stress levels decrease. Decreased stress leads to a healthier life according to the results of scientific research. When we hold onto unforgiveness, rumination, and rehearsal of offenses, it drains our energy, wears down our immune systems, and we are vulnerable to becoming ill. "A tranquil heart gives life to the flesh, but envy makes the bones rot" (Prov. 14:30).

Increased Ability to Trust

One of God's character traits is faithfulness. When you put your trust in someone, you want that person to be faithful to you and the promises, contracts, covenants, or agreements you have. "Trust in the Lord with all your heart, and do not lean on your own understanding" (Prov. 3:5).

When we trust God, he will reward us for believing in him even though we have never seen him face-to-face (John 20:29). If we don't forgive, it means we don't trust God to take care of us and act on the situation. We rely on our own limited understanding, which leads to many mistakes. When we allow him to employ his infinite, all-knowing wisdom and understanding, not only do we conserve our energy, but we have the honor of watching him move in miraculous ways that we could never have conceived.

Receiving the Holy Spirit and God's Power

"Repent and be baptized every one of you in the name of Jesus Christ for the forgiveness of sins, and you will receive the gift of the Holy Spirit" (Acts 2:38). This is one of the scriptural commands with a promise. This verse indicates that there is no lag time between accepting Christ and being filled with Holy Spirit. Many believers think that the two processes are mutually exclusive, but they are not. The new believer is immediately endued with the same power and authority that a long-time believer has. Our authority comes from our relationship with Jesus Christ. Yet we cannot have power in God without his Holy Spirit dwelling inside of us. The Holy Spirit is pure and cannot live inside a dirty vessel. Once we are washed clean inside and out by the blood of Christ, then the Spirit comes to fill us.

Learning to Forgive Ourselves As We Forgive Others

"And a second is like it: You shall love your neighbor as yourself" (Matt. 22:39). We cannot love without forgiveness. The two godly concepts go hand in hand. God first loved us then provided forgiveness for us. We first love ourselves, and then we can love others. This can be applied to forgiveness as well. We forgive ourselves first and then can forgive others. An entire chapter will be devoted to the issue of self-forgiveness later in this book.

Helping and Blessing Others

Pharaoh pled with Moses to pray and ask God to forgive his sins on one occasion. Moses did as he requested, and God did end the plague of locusts in Egypt. "Now therefore forgive my sin, please, only this once, and plead with the LORD your God only to remove this death from me" (Exod. 10:17).

Helping others first, in God's universe, guarantees that we will get our needs met as well. Forgiving others releases forgiveness for our sins. Interceding for the forgiveness of others also releases blessings of forgiveness for us.

Learning to Apologize

"Please forgive the trespass of your servant" (1 Sam. 25:28). This is one of the least addressed issues in the church today, other than sex. Yet, unlike the sex issue, forgiveness is not taboo but seems to be purposefully overlooked due to stubborn willfulness of man. We all require forgiveness from God and our fellow human beings once in a while, and that is okay. We have all sinned and fallen short of God's perfection. There is not one person who is an exception. Learning to be humble is learning to be like Christ. "For by grace you have been saved through faith. And this is not your own doing; it is the gift of God, not a result of works, so that no one may boast" (Eph. 2:8–9).

Secular Benefits of Forgiving

Fewer Trauma Symptoms

(Johnston 2008)

A correlational study of adult females who had posttraumatic stress disorder (PTSD) symptoms following a sexual trauma was conducted by this author. Although the number of participants was small, the results indicated that there was a significant correlation within groups for PTSD symptoms and the ability to forgive. The between group difference was significant (an inverse relationship) for those who stated that they had forgiven the perpetrator/s compared to those who had not forgiven their perpetrator/s. Also, those who had a religious affiliation found it harder to forgive the perpetrator/s than those who stated they had no religious affiliation. I surmised that those with a religious affiliation had a deeper sense of injustice and restitution based upon their belief systems, whereas those who were not spiritual may have used other coping skills such as trying to cover the offense without really dealing with it. In addition, those who stated that they had no religious affiliation and had forgiven the perpetrator/s had experienced their sexual trauma at very young ages prior to developing a sense of awareness of the assault or a sense of justice or injustice, or at an age when they could express the offense/s with cognitive maturity and the use of language.

Forgiveness Is Difficult

(Johnston 2011)

In an empirically based study of nonclinical graduate students, the difference between forgiveness therapy and narrative therapy was compared. A collaborative, brief workshop format was employed. I discovered that most of the participants held inaccurate conceptions of forgiveness, which they held onto throughout the workshop, particularly where personal forgiveness was concerned. There were no significant changes in the ability to forgive an offender; although the participants stated at the end of the workshop that they felt certain they were capable of employing forgiveness as a therapeutic method in their professional practices. A follow-up research question is, "Can an unforgiving therapist assist a client in learning to forgive?"

Increased Empathy

(Farrow et al. 2005, 2001; Toussaint and Webb 2005)

Research involving brain scans in England has shown promising results in support of forgiveness as a treatment for trauma symptoms. Both studies cited above were performed in the emergency department of a single hospital. Researchers were attempting to find a region in the brain that can be identified with forgiveness. What they discovered was that areas of the brain related to social cognition (empathy) and forgiveness are simultaneously activated and that there is increased PTSD resolution in individuals who exhibit empathy for an offender.

A hypothesis of the study was that there may be possible gender differences and the ability to forgive based on empathy. The researchers discovered that women are more empathetic than men while there were no gender differences for forgiving even though there was a significant association between empathy and forgiveness. There was no association between empathy and forgiveness for women, which contradicts the data collected during the brain scans. The more empathic men were, the more forgiving they were. The less empathic men were, the less forgiving they were. Does this mean that women's brains process forgiveness differently than men's brains or that women process forgiveness in a different region of the brain than men?

Enhanced Capacity to Trust

(Noll 2005)

This longitudinal forgiveness study was conducted with adolescent females who had been sexually abused by their mothers' male partners. The participants were chosen based upon their mental health symptoms including depression, PTSD symptoms, and the broken trust in the relationship with their mother and the offender. Forgiveness was so powerful that the adolescents, who were able to complete their forgiveness journeys, were prepared to reconcile with their offenders and had to be warned not to do so. The researcher also found that girls who were able to forgive developed higher self-esteem, less anxiety, better relationships with their mothers, and fewer symptoms of PTSD.

Freedom from the Control of Past Events

(Witvliet, Phipps, Feldman, and Beckham 2004)

A dispositional study done by Witvliet, Phipps, Feldman, and Beckham (2004) asserts that veterans who had difficulty forgiving themselves, others, and/or God suffered higher blood pressure and heart rates, as well as greater levels of anxiety, depression, and more intense PTSD symptoms than veterans who were able to forgive. Veterans who had healthy religious associations, who were willing to work through problems hand in hand with God and who sought spiritual support, had fewer PTSD symptoms.

Greater Sense of Empowerment and Mastery

(Luskin 2005)

A forgiveness study with a nonclinical population of college students who had experienced an interpersonal offense found that a forgiveness intervention focused on changing thought processes (cognitive reframing) greatly improved certain aspects of the participants' emotional and behavioral coping skills. Specifically, as the tendency to forgive increased, the willingness to forgive increased, and the degree of hurt and anger decreased. Positive outcomes of the intervention included a greater degree of focus on the future, development of self-efficacy, as well as spiritual growth.

Improved Overall Physical Health

(Witvliet, Ludwig, Vander Laan 2001; Witvliet 2005; Worthington, Jr., Witvliet, Pietrini, Miller 2007)

These studies found that when individuals forgave an offender, their well-being indices increased dramatically, they became more altruistic (helping others) and cooperative in general. They improved even more when they had the opportunity to discuss the offense with the offender face-to-face. Improvements in well-being included improved cardiovascular health, peripheral physiology, and brain physiology.

Significant Improvement in Psychiatric Disorders

(Berry, Worthington, O'Connor, Parrott, and Wade 2005)

Researchers studying forgiveness from a moral perspective found that it had a positive impact on the offended person in terms of lasting physical health, psychological functioning, and creating better social adjustment. The researchers also found that forgiveness had lasting global implications.

Decreased Unforgiveness

(Wade and Worthington 2003)

Although some individuals are able to clearly state they have forgiven an offense, others feel that they cannot or have not forgiven their offender. It is as though forgiveness is on a spectrum from low-forgiveness ability to high-forgiveness ability. If an individual does not feel like s/he has forgiven an offender, for example, does that really mean s/he has not forgiven? In other words, forgiveness may be polarized, black-and-white, or all-or-none. This study found that individuals who could state that at the time of the study they had less unforgiveness toward their offender still experienced benefits similar to individuals who believed they had completely forgiven the offender.

Conclusion

The results of the secular research support the Word of God in the benefits received from forgiving: improved physical health, improved emotional health, improved mental health, decreased unforgiveness, increased ability to forgive, increased compassion, increased empathy, enhanced ability to trust, and empowerment. God provided for all our needs before the world was created, and whether or not the world sees or understands, it is longing for what only the Father can provide. Forgiveness is the foundation of Christianity, and increased support of biblical teaching is coming to light.

6

Who Should Forgive?

THE SCRIPTURES ARE not jaded. All people are to forgive one another as we already have been forgiven. There is not one person who cannot be forgiven. The best example of this is Adolph Hitler. Had he asked for forgiveness in Christ, it would have been granted. How can that be? We are equal in the sight of God. In our human domain, we rank offenses and their punishments by severity; our justice system requires that the punishment fit the crime. Even the OT laws specify certain penalties for specific behaviors. Those laws were given for the sake of mankind. God views offenses in a different manner. His justice is of a higher order. When we begin to assign ranks or levels of forgiveness, we make decisions that only God can make in his supreme authority. "For all have sinned and fall short of the glory of God" (Rom. 3:23).

In the heavenly realm, all sins carry equal weight. To be a just God, he created a perfect justice system without flaws. The smallest lie carries the penalty of eternal death just as the sin of intentional murder. That is the reason we all need Christ.

> For by grace you have been saved through faith. And this is not your own doing; it is the gift of God, not a result of works, so that no one may boast. (Eph. 2:8–9)

> For Christ also suffered once for sins, the righteous for the unrighteous, that he might bring us to God, being put to death in the flesh but made alive in the spirit. (1 Pet. 3:18)

What are the consequences if we draw a boundary line around those who can be forgiven and exclude those who cannot be forgiven? Who would be outside that line? Who would make that decision? What if you end up outside the forgiveness line because of the choice made by someone who you offended? In a fair system, forgiveness is all-or-none. Whether the individual is a Christian or not, forgiveness is not easy, and that is the reason we are directed and commanded to forgive. Yet, is forgiveness easier for some individuals than others?

Personality Traits and the Ability to Forgive

Researchers question whether forgiveness is an innate dispositional trait, depends upon external circumstances, or is contingent upon natural and environmental factors. There are people who have an easier time forgiving than others, and personality traits appear to be directly or indirectly influential. Roberts (1995) created the term *forgivingness* to define the natural dispositional trait or natural ability to forgive. In 2004, Brown studied the innate trait of narcissism in conjunction with forgivingness. He found that individuals who were low in dispositional forgiveness were more vengeful than individuals who were high in dispositional forgiveness. The most vengeful individuals were those who were the most narcissistic or excessively self-loving.

Berry et al. (2005) later modified the term *forgivingness* into *unforgivingness* as a description of people who were naturally more unforgiving. He differentiated between single acts of forgiving versus the innate trait of forgiveness. An analysis by Berry of four different forgiveness studies confirmed the research expectations in each case; "negative affective traits (neuroticism, trait anger, hostility, depression, and fear) correlated with unforgiveness while positive affective traits (agreeableness, empathetic concern, perspective-taking, and extraversion) correlated with the ability to forgive" (p. 213). In that same study, vengeful rumination was associated with perpetuating negative emotions triggered by the event, which in turn perpetuate unforgiveness while inhibiting forgiveness.

Conclusion

In conclusion, everyone is commanded to forgive. Although research indicates that there are some people who have personality traits that make it easier for them to forgive. Some people have natural personality traits that make it more difficult for them to successfully forgive. Some of the traits that make forgiving difficult are narcissism, low self-esteem, shyness, embarrassment, and loneliness. Second, the closer two people are in a relationship, the easier it is to forgive one another, which may surprise some readers. Lastly, each individual who has been offended can make the choice to either ruminate (rehearse) the offense to keep the memory alive or to let go of the memory and move on with life.

Exercise

What is your definition of forgiveness? _____

_____

_____

_____

_____

Are there some offenses that are unforgiveable? _____

_____

What are they? _____

_____

_____

_____

_____

Are some people incapable of forgiving? _____

_____

_____

Do you easily forgive? _____

_____

Who decides when a person is offended? _____

_____

Who decides when a person is ready to forgive? _____

_____

Why is that true for you? _____

_____

_____

_____

_____

How do you decide who to forgive? _____

_____

_____

_____

How do you decide when to forgive? _____

_____

_____

_____

_____

Who should never be forgiven? _____

_____

7

Who Should Not Forgive?

ULTIMATELY EVERYONE IS commanded to forgive. Let's review what forgiveness is *not*. True forgiveness does not look for reasons to be offended. It does not use forgiveness as a weapon or bring up constant reminders of the offense. That means the offender does not owe you anything for your forgiveness. It is a clean slate when the matter is concluded. The injured person also gives up the right to continually bring up the fact that s/he has forgiven the offender. That is a form of retaliation, not forgiveness. True forgiveness is also not smug self-righteousness. The injured person is not better than the offender. Remember that we have all sinned and need God's forgiveness.

If you are exhibiting any of the above behaviors, you are not forgiving. It is just as wrong to punish the offender with false forgiveness as it was for them to offend you. It is healthier to admit that you are still hurt, angry, and not ready to forgive. In that way, you are not adding injustices onto the situation and not giving the offender a reason to appear to be the actual victim.

Forgive when you are ready and can make an honest attempt. If you start the forgiveness process and have to quit for a time, that is all right. You may even need to revisit the definition and details about forgiveness. You can start again.

Note: individuals who have been deeply traumatized are not immediately candidates for forgiveness therapy until they (1) have resolved some of the trauma, (2) have shown resilience, (3) have learned coping skills, and (4) have a support group.

Forgiveness Readiness Questionnaire

1) When you think about the offense, what are your automatic thoughts?

_____

_____

2) When you think about the offense, how do you feel?

_____

_____

3) When you think about the offense, what do you do, or what would you like to do?

_____

_____

4) When you think about the offender, what are your automatic thoughts?

_____

_____

5) When you think about the offender, how do you feel?

_____

_____

6) When you think about the offender, what do you do, or what would you like to do?

_____

_____

7) On a scale of 1–10 (1 is lowest, 10 is highest), what was the severity of the offense? _____

8) Are you ready to forgive the offender? _____

9) Are you ready to completely release the offender from all debts owed to you? _____

10) Do you believe the offender still owes restitution for the offense? _____

11) Do you keep reminding the offender about the offense? _____

12) Do you know the offender? _____

13) What was your relationship to the offender prior to the offense? _____

14) Are you prepared to find compassion toward the offender? _____

15) So do you have coping skills that will help you during the forgiveness process? _____

16) Will you have support during the forgiveness process? _____

8

◆

What Is the Danger in Forgiving?

THE RESEARCH INDICATES that using forgiveness as part of psychotherapy has never injured anyone. Occasionally, enthusiastic practitioners make therapeutic decisions that can be harmful to clients but forgiveness itself is not harmful. There are a number of strategies that can be used to safeguard clients.

The first is to remember that forgiveness is for the injured person, not the offender, although that person may also benefit. The process is not meant to harm or reinjure the offended person. Second, do not use the term *victim*. Many survivors of trauma are offended just by the thought of being a helpless victim. Also, for individuals who have experienced deep trauma, precautions must be taken. The incident is now a memory, and the person is only responding to something that happened in the past. The injured person is to be reminded that s/he is in the here and now, and the pain is coming from leftover emotional and physical sensations. They may appear very real, but the hurt is in the past. Obviously, this is not the case when people are living in an abusive or dangerous place, and where repeated offenses are currently occurring.

One of the problems with forgiveness arises when an individual is in a place (at least temporarily) where s/he is faced with active long-term abuse as well as the abuser. Abused children generally live for years with, or are cared for by, their perpetrator/s. Spouses may find themselves trapped in abusive marriages. Individuals who rely on others to care for them, such as the elderly or those living with disabilities, may be trapped in abusive relationships with their caretakers. Adult children may find themselves caring for abusive elderly parents.

How does forgiveness apply to these individuals? How can anyone tell victims and survivors of extreme trauma and injustice that they need to forgive because it will benefit them when they are suffering, and there is no end in sight? Only the power of God can reach down and help those individuals. He may use us as a resource.

For those individuals who may be living with daily trauma and are not able to leave the situation, safety is the first priority. Forgiveness is of no value if it puts the person in harm's way. The person who is experiencing current trauma may not believe that God loves her/him. Be God's reminder to that person that he does love his children. Prayer is a powerful weapon (James 5:16).

Forgiveness therapy and trauma resolution employed with children, particularly those who have been or are being abused, must move slowly. Figure out ways to explain forgiveness to them so that they don't feel shame or guilt or increased anger. Monitor the child's automatic thoughts and note if s/he is taking responsibility for the situation rather than appropriately placing the responsibility on the offender. Use of word pictures, puppets, or games helps facilitate the forgiveness process. Children also have a natural, inborn, God-given ability to forgive. When they do forgive, it is very powerful. As noted in the study by Noll (2005), a child or an adolescent who forgives may want to reconcile with a person who is dangerous. They need close monitoring during the forgiveness process to remain safe.

Forgiveness is not for the weak because it takes courage to grant mercy in exchange for an injustice. It can be likened to a coupon. You trade something worthless (a piece of paper) for something of value (a monetary discount on a purchase or a free item). It is our worthlessness and sin exchanged for the precious life and blood of Jesus Christ.

9

Forgiveness Stories

**"I never have a problem forgiving.
I just do it automatically."**

PEOPLE WHO BELIEVE that they can automatically forgive without going through a forgiveness process do not fully understand what forgiveness is. The most confident forgivers tend to discover that they are not actually practicing forgiveness but are burying their true feelings or using unhealthy coping mechanisms to avoid thinking about the offense. They may be holding erroneous beliefs that have been passed down in the family or have unwittingly developed their own functional/dysfunctional ideas of forgiveness. There are, of course, very minor issues that one can easily get over. True offenses of a deeper nature will require work and conscious processing of the offense.

"I guess I haven't forgiven them after all."

During a forgiveness group I facilitated in the addiction community a number of years ago, a middle-aged woman shared her ease of forgiving the people who had deeply traumatized her. Her offenders had all been family members. She felt confident that her life was healed, and she expressed a carefree attitude about the past. As she learned the definition of evidence-based forgiveness, she seemed uncertain. She began to see the connection between her own addiction to substances and her unresolved trauma issues. Suddenly, she blurted out, "I thought I had forgiven them because they are all dead. I guess I haven't forgiven them after all!"

She realized what she had been feeling was a sense of satisfaction because her offenders were no longer living. Yet, she was drowning her pain underneath the alcohol she consumed. In fact, her addiction had started in adolescence during the time of her abuse. She discovered that she had much work to do, and her forgiveness journey was just beginning.

"I can't remember his name."

During one of my professional presentations, a gentleman approached me and shared that his wife had been involved in a severe auto accident a number of years earlier. Her injuries were so bad that she was hospitalized for more than a year and required many surgeries to be able to function normally again. He recounted thinking about the accident and the other driver who had caused it every day. During my presentation, he realized that he could no longer remember the name of the other driver! The gentleman was shocked to discover that he really had forgiven the other driver and had no ill feelings toward him any longer.

"Was it enough?"

During a men's self-forgiveness group, one of the participants shared a story about deep betrayal he was currently experiencing. He admitted that he was complicit in the offense and had exhibited behaviors that led to the start of the situation. He no longer had joint custody of his daughter nor was he able to see her. He discovered that his daughter was calling the man his former girlfriend was living with "daddy." His shame and guilt were so deep that he assaulted the man who was helping raise his young daughter. The assault was so severe that the man he attacked almost died. After he had recounted his story, I asked one question, "Was it enough?" The room became silent. His response was, "No. Nothing would have been enough." At that moment he had incredible insight. No amount of revenge can satisfy us when we have been hurt. Nothing we can do, and nothing our offenders can do, really makes up for an offense against us. Nor can we do enough to make up for the offenses we commit against others. Only forgiveness can heal the pain we experience from deep offenses.

"How do I forgive someone who is dead?"

Forgiveness is *not* dependent upon an apology. Why not? Most offenders will never apologize. You could spend your entire life waiting to be released by an offender for whom you have unforgiveness. All those years would be spent carrying a burden that is unnecessary and only burdens you. This is evident in a simple example.

A question that many clients have asked me is, "How do I forgive someone who is dead?" That is one of the reasons we forgive regardless of the apology. We are in control of ourselves and our decisions. The moment we allow someone else to control us, we become their slave. The ability to forgive is a gift from God. He trusts us to use that power for our good and the good of others. We do not forgive for their sake, as some researchers have suggested, but we forgive for our benefit and the offenders' benefit vicariously. It is a beautiful paradox. That is the example we have in Christ. His sacrifice by which we experience forgiveness is a free gift.

"Can I forgive on behalf of someone else?"

What is an offense? Who decides when an offense has been committed? Since we have free will, we are able to make choices about the things that are said or done to us. Each person has the right to make the decision about what is or is not an offense and when an offense has been committed. Is it the right of one person to feel offended on behalf of another? Would the unforgiveness of one person block the ability of another to forgive?

A mother shared with me her concern for her twenty-one-year-old daughter who was dating a young man who had been unfaithful to her daughter. The daughter had forgiven her boyfriend, and their relationship moved forward. The mother had made the decision to ban her daughter from dating the young man any longer because she herself was unable to forgive him. Apart from the fact that her daughter would only desire the relationship more when her mother forbade it, I wondered whether or not this mother would eventually create a regrettable situation that would be even worse. I agreed that she had a parental responsibility to advise her daughter. Yet, if her adult daughter made the decision to forgive, was it right for her mother to influence her by attempting to hold onto an issue that the couple had already resolved? Fortunately, in the end, the mother was able to overcome her negative feelings toward the young man and made the decision not only to forgive him but also to make the effort to get to know him better.

"Do I have to work so hard every day at forgiving?"

A client, who was battling addictions, asked this in group treatment one day. She was laboring intensely to forgive a long list of people who had traumatized her in childhood and adolescence. The whole process seemed daunting and unachievable. In fact, she had given up hope and given up her forgiveness work.

My response to her was that there will always be forgiveness work to perform. Some of the work takes a greater amount of time, and some is simpler. I urged her to give herself a break periodically and put the forgiveness issues aside. In fact, I suggest that clients put the offenses and offenders in an imaginary box for a period of time. Then when they are ready to do more work, they can open the box and start again.

"I don't know what just happened, but something did."

One of the exercises that I perform within group therapy is to direct the participants to complete a form with the offenders' names and their offenses written on them. I ask the participants to sign the documents. They either tear the documents into small pieces and throw them away or burn them in a barrel.

When they burn them in the barrel, the clients usually spontaneously hold hands or put their arms around one another's shoulders and gather around the barrel. As the flames and ash fly into the air, the participants watch in silence. Some of them wander off alone to contemplate for a time. A comment that is expressed nearly every time this exercise if performed is that there is a feeling of freedom. They don't know why they feel different, but the symbolic release of the offenders and the offenses lifts the burden of unforgiveness that weighs each one down. Even if the feeling goes away and thoughts of unforgiveness creep back in, the participants have that memory as evidence that they made the decision to forgive and let go.

10

Hindrances and Facilitators
of Forgiveness

<u>What Makes Forgiveness Difficult?</u>	<u>What Makes Forgiveness Easy?</u>
Not receiving an apology	Family
Not being believed	Justice
Not being respected	Reciprocity
Seeing the offender regularly	Restitution
Repetitive injury by the offender	Apology
Fear	Being heard
Bitterness	Being understood
	Faith, spirituality, religion
	Personality traits

Hatred	Self-esteem
Lack of insight	Self-efficacy
Lack of compassion	Empowerment
Self-pity	Control over life
Substance abuse	Positive role models
Mental illness	Positive coping skills
Narcissism	Safety
Lack of role positive role models	Security
	Love
Immaturity	Support
Age	Good relationship prior to offense
Gender	
Culture, society	Severity of the offense

STUDY THE ABOVE lists. Which factors are making it difficult for you to forgive yourself? Which of those factors are making it difficult for you to forgive others? Which of the factors in the second list facilitate your ability to forgive yourself and others? Take time to make your own list and be specific. Be detailed. How can you change those factors yourself so that your life is lining up with the commands of God?

Telling someone to "just get over it" or "just forgive" does not work. Trying harder does not work. There are specific methods for forgiving. One will be addressed at the end of this text. If you truly want to practice forgiveness, make the time to do the work that it requires. Over time, you will get better at it.

My facilitators

_____

_____

_____

_____

_____

_____

_____

My hindrances

_____

_____

_____

_____

_____

_____

_____

_____

11

How to Forgive

THE BIBLE TELLS us how to forgive in a step-by-step manner.

1. Remember that God is your Father. He created you. "For you formed my inward parts; you knitted me together in my mother's womb" (Ps. 139:13).

2. Remember that God alone has authority over your life. He has a plan for your life. "For I am sure that neither death nor life, nor angels nor rulers, nor things present nor things to come, nor powers, nor height nor depth, nor anything else in all creation, will be able to separate us from the love of God in Christ Jesus our Lord" (Rom. 8:38–39).

3. Focus on his love for you. Even when you are emotionally disturbed, hold onto that fact. Thank him for all the good things he has done for you.

4. Meditate on Jesus' death at Calvary for the forgiveness of your sins. Thank him for dying in your place and for your forgiveness. Thank him that you have eternal life.

5. Give up (relinquish) all debts owed to you by the offender.

6. Continue to forgive the person, even if you have to do it 70 x 7 times.

7. Pray for the offender whether the person is a believer or an unbeliever. Think about the offender's life and possible motives for hurting you.

8. When you are tempted to take the offense back again, remember how awful it feels to not be forgiven. Open your hands and give your pain to God.

9. Remind yourself that your healing is connected to forgiving rather than the offender.

10.Remind yourself that you received the Holy Spirit when you accepted Christ for the forgiveness of your sins. You have the power of that same Holy Spirit living and operating inside of you today to help you forgive yourself and others.

Forgiveness Exercise No. 1

Goals: To practice forgiving using the concepts from this text.

Objectives:

1. Understand what forgiveness is and is not.
2. Understand the positive impact forgiveness can have on one's life.
3. Give the gift of mercy to someone.
4. Discover your personal benefits of forgiving.

Strategies:

1. Find forgiveness scriptures from God's Word that apply to your situation. Write them on a note card, and place them where you can see them every day (on the refrigerator, on the bathroom mirror, on your pillow, etc.). Speak those verses aloud when you see them.
2. Spend time praying before you begin. Tell God what you are feeling and experiencing during the process. If this takes more than one day, pray before starting each time.

3. Write about your personal ideas/concepts of forgiveness.

4. Write, in detail, a story about a time when you forgave someone.

5. Write, in detail a story about someone you are in the process of forgiving.

6. Write, in detail, a story about someone you believe you cannot or will not forgive.

7. Compare the stories, and record the differences between them. For instance, how and why did you successfully forgive someone compared to what you still need to do to forgive an offender? Or, what are you doing to forgive someone right now, compared to why you believe you cannot forgive someone else.

8. Then write a detailed story about a time when someone forgave you, and what it was like to attempt to receive the gift of mercy rather than to "get what you deserved."

9. Compare the difference between your forgiveness of someone else and the time when someone forgave you. Include the struggles, the reason for a failed attempt, why you should receive forgiveness when someone else should not, etc.

10. Re-write your forgiveness story so that you are not a victim but a successful victor.

Forgiveness Exercise No. 2

Automatic Thought Record

Think of an offense that has occurred in your life recently. Record the offense. Then record the erroneous beliefs you had in the second column. Then, for each belief, record the consequence, the dispute, and the new thought. You may have multiple beliefs, consequences, disputes, and new beliefs for a single activating event.

Offense	Erroneous Belief	Consequence	Dispute	Effective New Thought

Forgiveness Exercise No. 3

Keep a daily record of the following for four weeks.

Number of times per day you think about the offense	How you feel when you think about the offense	Number of times a day you think about the offender	How you feel when you think about the offender

Forgiveness Exercise No. 4

Does anything relieve the negative feelings from the offense? _____

What do you do to cope? _____

_____

_____

_____

_____

_____

_____

_____

_____

If you do not have a coping method, consider the following:

1. Stop the negative thoughts.
   a. Interrupting: do something that will shock you out of the rumination. Try sucking on a lemon, dropping an ice cube down your clothing, working out hard, or snapping a rubber band on the inside of your wrist.
   b. Redirecting: think about something important you need to accomplish, or someone else who deserves more of your time.

    c. Distracting: focus on finding a solution rather than ruminating on the problem.

2. Evaluate the thoughts
   a. Are they beneficial to me?
   b. Do they make me feel good?
   c. Do they benefit someone else?
   d. Do they help me meet my goals?

3. Replace the thoughts
   a. Reframe the thoughts into positive ones: make an effort to turn the thought 180 degrees in the opposite direction. Example: Instead of thinking about how much you dislike the offender or the offense, tell yourself there was a reason for what happened, and learn from the experience.
   b. Purposefully think about something positive: Find something positive about the offender even if the person is a stranger to you. Imagine what may have motivated the offender to do what s/he did. Work to find compassion for the offender.
   c. Meditate on scripture: find a Bible verse that applies to the situation, and ruminate on it rather than the offense.

4. Set new goals
    a. Your life may have changed since the offense. Create a new pattern for yourself. Start a new diet plan, join a gym, start a new craft project, join a support group, or take up a new hobby. Change something in your life that you have control over which will take you down a new path away from what happened.

Forgiveness Exercise No. 5

Choosing to Forgive

Choose a person who you are ready to forgive. At this point, you are making a conscious commitment to go through with the forgiveness process and hold onto forgiveness even when it is difficult.

Light a candle to light the path of forgiveness. Write the name of the person you wish to forgive.

I forgive: _____

_____

What I am forgiving:

_____

_____

_____

_____

_____

_____

12

Self-Forgiveness Exercises

Self-Forgiveness Exercise No. 1

Goals: Learning that forgiving others can be connected to the ability to forgive oneself and vice versa. This is a group assignment but can also be performed by individuals.

Objectives:

1. Learn self-value even in the face of making choices or acting out behavior that lead to negative consequences for oneself or others.
2. Learn the value of granting oneself forgiveness.
3. Learn the value of granting oneself compassion.

Strategies:

1. Who is the most difficult person to forgive?
2. Discuss with the group or consider on your own the difficulty with self-forgiveness versus forgiving others. Ask, "Can we truly be free to forgive others when we cannot or will not forgive ourselves?"
3. Each group member will share a personal item (i.e., photo, ring, letter, and book) with the group that defines, describes, or reflects the individual. If you are doing this exercise by yourself, choose an item that you own that represents you, and journal your answers. Members will tell the story about the item and how it came to be important, as well as how it reveals something about them by considering the following:

   a. What does this item say about me?
   b. Why is this important to me?
   c. Where did this item come from, and how did I come to possess it (i.e., did I purchase it, find it, or was it a gift?)?

4. The group will finish with a discussion about self-worth in the face of individual humanness. The group members will explore extending forgiveness

and compassion to themselves as well as receiving it. Emphasize the importance of receiving forgiveness and moving on with life after a period of repentance, remorse, or atonement. Use the following questions to facilitate the process:

a. How does it feel to consider forgiving you?
b. What sensations do you feel in your body?
c. Is it comfortable or uncomfortable?
d. What might be blocking it?

Self-Forgiveness Exercise No. 2

Complete the chart below with any negative automatic thoughts that you have about you.

Schema	Explanation	Example
Arbitrary inferences	Making a judgment with no supporting inferences	
Overgeneralization	Making a broad rule with little support	
Catastrophizing	Blowing something out of proportion	
Labeling/mislabeling	Attaching a negative label to yourself after a negative experience	

Dichotomous or polarized thinking/ all-or-none/ black-and-white	Categorizing things into one of two extremes	
Personalize	Attributing an event to yourself when there is actually little supporting evidence	
Selective abstraction/ conclusion/ isolated detail	Making a judgment based on limited information while ignoring other information	

Self-Forgiveness Exercise No. 3

> By this we shall know that we are of the truth and reassure our heart before him; for whenever our heart condemns us, God is greater than our heart, and he knows everything. (1 John 3:19–20)

When God no longer condemns us, what right do we have to condemn ourselves?

_____

What did God do to forgive you?

_____

How can you show God that you honor his son's sacrifice?

_____

Describe a time in your life when you forgave someone.

_____

Describe a time in your life when someone forgave you.

_____

How did it feel to forgive someone else?

_____

How did it feel to be forgiven?

_____

Self-Forgiveness Exercise No. 4

What is self-forgiveness? It is accepting yourself with all your human attributes and faults. It means letting go of anger toward yourself for past failures and mistakes. It means no longer needing penance, sorrow, self-inflicted punishment, or grieving for a past mistake. Self-forgiveness is the act of compassion given to you and received by you. It involves spiritual, emotional, and psychological self-healing. It involves unconditional self-acceptance and letting go of the burden of guilt. Without self-forgiveness, you will continue to wallow in failure, which will hold you back from becoming the person you want to be. Whether or not others forgive you for what you have done, it is vital that you find it within yourself to take control of your freedom.

I am making an offer of forgiveness to myself (insert your own name). I release myself from the act below by granting mercy to myself, which I also freely receive. I understand that God forgives my sins, and I have no legal right to hold anything against myself either.

_____

I am forgiving (name the specific act):

_____

_____

_____

I agree to receive/accept the forgiveness offered to me (sign your name below):

_____

Self-Forgiveness Exercise No. 5

Number of times per day you think about your offenses	How you feel when you think about the offenses	Number of times a day you think about your offenses	How you feel when you think about yourself

Self-Forgiveness Exercise No. 6

What does God say about me? Speak these verses to yourself daily for thirty days. Record your responses below before beginning this project and again at the end of the thirty days.

How do I feel about me at this time (do I love myself, do I respect myself, do I believe in myself)?

_____

_____

How do I behave toward me (do I take care of my health, do I take time alone to relax, am I working in a job that I like)?

_____

_____

How do I think about me at this time (do I believe that I'm a failure, do I think that I am a good person, do I see others as better than me)?

_____

_____

Before I formed you in the womb I knew you, and before you were born I consecrated you; I appointed you a prophet to the nations. (Jer. 1:5)

For in Christ Jesus you are all sons of God, through faith. (Gal. 3:26)

Therefore, if anyone is in Christ, he is a new creation. The old has passed away; behold, the new has come. (2 Cor. 5:17)

For we are his workmanship, created in Christ Jesus for good works, which God prepared beforehand, that we should walk in them. (Eph. 2:10)

I do not ask for these only, but also for those who will believe in me through their word, that they may all be one, just as you, Father, are in me, and I in you, that they also may be in us, so that the world may believe that you have sent me. The glory that you have given me I have given to them, that they may be one even as we are one, I in them and you in me, that they may become perfectly one, so that the world may know that you sent me and loved them even as you loved me. Father, I desire that they also, whom you have given me, may be with me where I am, to see my glory that you have given me because you loved me before the foundation of the world. (John 17:20–26)

For I know the plans I have for you, declares the Lord, plans for welfare and not for evil, to give you a future and a hope. (Jer. 29:11)

For you formed my inward parts; you knitted me together in my mother's womb. I praise you, for I am fearfully and wonderfully made. Wonderful are your works; my soul knows it very well. My frame was not hidden from you, when I was being made in secret, intricately woven in the depths of the earth. Your eyes saw my unformed substance; in your book were written, every one of them, the days that were formed for me, when as yet there was none of them. (Ps. 139:13–16)

Do you not know that you are God's temple and that God's Spirit dwells in you? If anyone destroys God's temple, God will destroy him. For God's temple is holy, and you are that temple. (1 Cor. 3:16–17)

No longer do I call you servants, for the servant does not know what his master is doing; but I have called you friends, for all that I have heard from my Father I have made known to you. (John 15:15)

So you are no longer a slave, but a son, and if a son, then an heir through God. (Gal. 4:7)

But to all who did receive him, who believed in his name, he gave the right to become children of God. (John 1:12)

But our citizenship is in heaven, and from it we await a Savior, the Lord Jesus Christ. (Phil. 3:20)

But you are a chosen race, a royal priesthood, a holy nation, a people for his own possession, that you may proclaim the excellencies of him who called you out of darkness into his marvelous light. (1 Pet. 2:9)

You shall be a crown of beauty in the hand of the Lord, and a royal diadem in the hand of your God. You shall no more be termed Forsaken, and your land shall no more be termed Desolate, but you shall be called My Delight Is in Her, and your land Married; for the Lord delights in you, and your land shall be married. For as a young man marries a young woman, so shall your sons marry you, and as the bridegroom rejoices over the bride, so shall your God rejoice over you. (Isa. 62:3–5)

There is therefore now no condemnation for those who are in Christ Jesus. For the law of the Spirit of life has set you free in Christ Jesus from the law of sin and death. (Rom. 8:1–2)

Little children, you are from God and have overcome them, for he who is in you is greater than he who is in the world. (1 John 4:4)

Keep me as the apple of your eye; hide me in the shadow of your wings. (Ps. 17:8)

Therefore, since we have been justified by faith, we have peace with God through our Lord Jesus Christ. (Rom. 5:1)

For God so loved the world, that he gave his only Son, that whoever believes in him should not perish but have eternal life. (John 3:16)

For by grace you have been saved through faith. And this is not your own doing; it is the gift of God. (Eph. 2:8)

No, in all these things we are more than conquerors through him who loved us. (Rom. 8:37)

So God created man in his own image, in the image of God he created him; male and female he created them. (Gen. 1:27)

Beloved, let us love one another, for love is from God, and whoever loves has been born of God and knows God. (1 John 4:7)

What does God say about me? Speak these verses to yourself daily for thirty days. Record your responses below before beginning this project and again at the end of the thirty days.

How do I feel about me at this time (do I love myself, do I respect myself, do I believe in myself)?

_____

_____

How do I behave toward me (do I take care of my health, do I take time alone to relax, am I working in a job that I like)?

_____

How do I think about me at this time (do I believe that I'm a failure, do I think that I am a good person, do I see others as better than me)?

THIRTY-ONE DAYS OF FORGIVENESS

A Forgiveness Study Guide

Testimony

AUTHORS TEND TO use their personal experiences as resources for encouraging, exhorting, and teaching. My life is no different. When I began my forgiveness journey, I was a young child. As I have matured, aged, and studied forgiveness, my concept of forgiveness has changed. What was once simple has become complex by nature. The following thirty-one steps of forgiveness will not necessarily move you to a place of forgiving those who have hurt you immediately, but it will change your thinking patterns in such a way that you will begin to change your attitudes and behavior. The companion books and workbooks will also increase your ability to forgive and find true freedom in Jesus.

I give all the glory to Abba (the Father God), the son (Jehovah), and the Holy Spirit for allowing me to come to this point in life, to have a foundation of knowledge, to have a deeper relationship with the Trinity, and to understand suffering and pain so that I can impart these words to you. "Then the angel showed me the river of the water of life, bright as crystal, flowing from the throne of God and the Lamb through the middle of the street of the city also, on either side of the river, the tree of life with its twelve kinds of fruit, yielding its fruit each month. The leaves of the tree were for the healing of the nations" (Rev. 22:1–2, ESV). The scripture also states in Luke 6:37–38, "Judge not, and you will not be judged; condemn not, and you will not be condemned; forgive, and you will be forgiven; give, and it will be given to you. Good measure, pressed down, shaken together, running over, will be put into your lap. For with the measure you use it will be measured back to you." When you forgive, you will receive forgiveness in good measure, pressed down, shaken together, running over, and measured back to you!

Day 1

> But with you there is forgiveness
> that you may be feared.

> —Psalm 130:4

What is the scripture saying to you?

_____

_____

_____

_____

What does it mean to fear God?

_____

_____

_____

_____

What is God's type of forgiveness compared to man's forgiveness?

_____

_____

_____

_____

God has provided forgiveness for every person who will ever live. He did that through his son, Jesus Christ (John 3:16). The forgiveness we find in our relationship with Jesus Christ is also referred to as grace in many places in the scripture. It is an indication of unearned favor with the one who created us to have an eternal relationship with Him. All our sins, past, present, and future are forgiven perpetually.

Fearing God is also called the beginning of wisdom (Ps. 111:10). The fear of the Lord is considered by many Bible scholars to include a sense of awe. How awesome it is to think that he sacrificed his one and only son to forgive all of us who have been disobedient and sinful. What human being would allow a group of evil people to scourge, torture, and crucify his son so that those very people could be forgiven? That is the awesome part about God's forgiveness.

He is so magnificent that he provided you with forgiveness that you don't deserve. You don't have to earn it but only believe.

Day 2

> If my people who are called by my name
> humble themselves, and pray and seek
> my face and turn from their wicked ways,
> then I will hear from heaven and will
> forgive their sin and heal their land.
>
> —2 Chronicles 7:14

What does it mean to be called by God's name?

_____

_____

_____

_____

Why can the land be healed only after the sins of the people are forgiven?

_____

_____

Asking for forgiveness requires that we admit we are sinful (wicked) by nature. Every action, behavior, or thought may not in itself be sinful, but our nature granted to us by Adam and Eve is inherently sinful. An important part of the whole forgiveness concept is that we understand we are *all* sinful (Rom. 3:23). We all sin each and every day. Understanding that every person is sinful also releases us to forgive others since no one can boast of being free from the sin nature or loftier than someone else.

Sin separates us from God and blocks our ability to constantly, freely seek Him, receive from him, and to feel comfortable in his presence. The promise in the verse above does not state that we have to try harder to earn forgiveness but that if we pray and seek him, he has provided the sin offering so that every barrier between him and us is removed. He provided the forgiveness in his power and authority. Then, when we are walking daily in his forgiveness, he is free to bless us by healing our government, our relationships, our businesses, our families, and our schools. It's our choice.

Day 3

> Consider my affliction and trouble
> and forgive all my sins.
>
> —Psalm 25:18

Why do we ask for forgiveness when we are in trouble or hurting?

_____

_____

_____

_____

Why is it difficult for Christians to admit mistakes or sins? When we initially come to God through the finished work of Jesus Christ on the cross, we come reverently, desperately, and as little children. The joy of our first forgiveness encounter with God can't be matched. What blocks us from continuing to joyfully seek and live in his forgiveness after that? Could it be true that our own sin might contribute at times to our afflictions, troubles, and hurts? Might we carry guilt and shame when we sin after we receive salvation? His forgiveness allows us to have eternal life yet, we may still suffer consequences in this life for our decisions and choices. It does not mean we intentionally sinned. Perhaps your affliction is due to the actions of someone else. Those who have been severely wounded may be in a place where self-examination is too painful. I am challenging you to ask God if there is anything in your life that is not part of him or of his plan. If you are living with hurt and trouble, ask God to forgive you for any part you had in creating it or sustaining it. When we know that we are forgiven, it allows us to trust in him to help us. Anything that is not of faith is sin (Rom. 14:23), and our trust in him is very important. Do we have the courage to admit when we are wrong? Do we need forgiveness in a situation where someone else wounded us, but we contributed in some way to our own victimization? Are we angry with God for what happened to us? God does not need our forgiveness, but we need his even in the midst of our affliction.

Day 4

> And no longer shall each one teach his
> neighbor and each his brother, saying, "Know
> the Lord," for they shall all know me, from
> the least of them to the greatest, declares
> the Lord. For I will forgive their iniquity,
> and I will remember their sin no more.
>
> —Jeremiah 31:34

What happens to your sin when you confess it to God?

_____

_____

_____

_____

What is the difference between iniquity and sin, or are they the same concept?

_____

The Greek word *hamartia* means "to miss the mark." This can be pictured as a marksman shooting an arrow or a bullet at a circular bull's-eye. Any shot that does not hit the direct center has missed the mark. So as Christians, our bull's-eye is every God-created law, commandment, and rule, which we must obey for our own benefit. Anytime that we miss the bull's-eye, we have committed a sin. Strong's dictionary (2010) defines sin as anything that falls short of the glory of God. This is a situational event. Strong defines iniquity as perversity and moral evil. Thus sin, when repeated against the knowledge of God, becomes transgression, which, if it continues long enough, transgression eventually becomes iniquity, which perverts the flesh. This perversion changes the DNA/RNA structure of the flesh and beliefs or attitudes resulting in genetic changes that are passed on from generation to generation. This is more serious and involves long-term, intentional rebelliousness against God. Yet, God provided forgiveness before we even knew Him or turned to him. That love is what draws us to him.

Day 5

> For you, O Lord, are good and
> forgiving, abounding in steadfast
> love to all who call upon you.
>
> —Psalm 86:5

What does forgiving have to do with love?

_____

_____

_____

_____

What does *steadfast* mean?

_____

_____

_____

_____

Forgiveness and love are connected with one another through the blood of Christ Jesus. God forgave you before you were born and before you ever committed a single sin. He provided forgiveness for you knowing that you would sin, rebel, and commit perverse acts against him. Only great and eternal love could plan and carry out such a sacrifice. Hatred of his creation would not motivate him to give us all that. Hatred would not allow people the option to choose eternal life over eternal death. The word *steadfast* (*Merriam-Webster* Online) carries with it the idea of a firm belief or to be firmly fixed in place. This means that even after you initially accept Christ as your savior, his shed blood continues to perpetually provide forgiveness for your sins.

Lastly, his plan is for everyone who will ever live to be forgiven. This plan is not just for a select few, who have some special characteristic or qualification. It is hard to fathom that he would forgive each one of us, let alone individuals who have committed what we consider heinous crimes. Yet his plan is perfect, and it must include all or none. In God's law, every missed bull's-eye carries equal weight regardless of man's laws.

Day 6

> For this is my blood of the covenant which is
> poured out for many for the forgiveness of sins.
>
> —Matthew 26:28

What is a blood covenant?

_____

_____

_____

_____

A covenant is a binding agreement between two parties (BibleGateway.com). Abraham cut the first covenant with God. Abraham had been directed to walk blamelessly before God, which he could not do. God required a blood covenant because life force is in the blood. The Hebrew word for covenant is *berith*, means "to cut", and Abraham was instructed to cut sacrificial animals in half and lay the halves across from one another (Gen. 15:8–10). When the sun set, God Almighty, in the form of a smoking firepot and flaming torch, passed between the pieces as a sign to Abraham of the covenant (Gen. 15:17). It meant that God required nothing of Abraham, but God would fulfill his half of the covenant regardless. The blood of animals was only a temporary answer to the problem and had to be repeated annually. The only way for God to make a permanent atonement on our behalf was to create an example of the Abrahamic covenant by sacrificing one who would make a permanent atonement for sin. He cleverly sent himself (Jesus) as a man to earth in human form with a free will to live a completely sinless life. Jesus became our Christ as the lamb who was slain and who shed his blood for us. It was for all mankind. Today we remember and honor his sacrifice by taking Communion. One drop of his heavenly, anointed blood would have been enough to forgive us, but he *poured* it out.

Day 7

> Indeed, under the law almost everything is purified
> with blood, and without the shedding of blood
> there is no forgiveness of sins.
>
> —Hebrews 9:22

Why did God require the shedding of blood for forgiveness of sins?

_____

_____

_____

_____

What makes blood pure?

_____

_____

_____

Living creatures are dependent upon blood to live. Initially, mankind was dependent upon blood in the natural realm. Because of sin, God required that something die so that something else could live. That blood covenant transferred into the realm of the supernatural, and forever God will see us covered in the righteousness of Christ because Jesus shed his blood as the atonement for our sins. He is referred to in scripture as the "lamb who takes away the sins of the world" (John 1:29).

Blood carried away from the heart by the arteries (with the exception of the pulmonary artery) is oxygen-rich blood. The veins carry the oxygen-depleted blood back toward the heart where it is renewed. When the Holy Spirit is working inside of us, he provides power from the oxygen-rich blood of Jesus Christ so that we can have forgiveness, direction and guidance, cast out devils, live in comfort and health, prophesy, speak in tongues, live holy lives without sin, have access to the Father, and live in purity, sanctification, justification, and liberty, and etc. This is the reason the bible states that the red blood of Christ is able to wash our garments whiter than snow (Isa. 1:18).

Day 8

> Therefore I tell you, her sins, which are many,
> are forgiven-for she loved much. But he who is
> forgiven little, loves little.

> —Luke 7:47

What came first, forgiveness or love?

_____

_____

_____

_____

In this scripture, the Father's love came first and forgiveness second. The woman's gift of forgiveness came first and then her love. God loved before we sinned, and he also had foreknowledge that we would sin. Yet he loved us. The provision of his sacrifice arose from his love toward us. Our love toward him results from his forgiveness of our sins first. He didn't have to love or forgive us. We can't do anything to make him love us or forgive us. We don't have to accept his forgiveness and love. He can't make us accept his forgiveness or love him. We learn to receive from him from a free will.

That means the covenant that was cut between God and man is heavily one-sided. God has done everything for us except mandate love from us or force us to accept forgiveness for our sins. When he makes a covenant, it is eternal, and he cannot break it. God's word is an eternal vow outside of time (Luke 21:33).

He is a just God and cannot break his own laws but made provision to keep his holy laws as well as save mankind from eternal damnation. God teaches us how to uphold justice and save the perpetrator at the same time. He also made the eternal leap outside of time to make a permanent contract with us, who live inside of time. He crossed the time barrier by coming to earth in the form of a man to pull us into eternity. The only conclusion we can come to is that he has great love for us that never ends.

Day 9

> And Peter said, "Repent and be baptized every
> one of you in the name of Jesus Christ for the
> forgiveness of your sins, and you will receive the
> gift of the Holy Spirit."
>
> —Acts 2:38

What does repentance have to do with forgiveness?

_____

_____

_____

_____

Why can't we receive the Holy Spirit until we initially repent?

_____

_____

God cannot and does not want to force us to repent or to love him. He desires that we come into a relationship of our own free will. Forced love is not satisfactory. His love for us is his free choice, and he waits for each of us to love him freely. Also, we can't receive forgiveness until we realize that we have a need for it. That was his intention for creating the Ten Commandments. It was meant to be a mirror held up to show us our sins, or missing the mark. Once we realize how difficult maintaining our own holiness is, we run to Him for eternal provision. Once we ask him to forgive our sins, we are then washed white from the red blood of Christ. Whenever God looks at us, he sees the righteousness provided by his son's sacrifice.

At that time, we are vessels worthy to receive the holiness of his spirit. Even though we will sin again and again, he continues to sanctify us so that we can learn through practice to use the gifts that come through the Holy Spirit. Whether our mistakes are intentional or unintentional, we are allowed to grow and mature at a pace that is unique to each one of us, and the Holy Spirit provides us with the power in his name.

Day 10

> Blessed are those whose lawless deeds are forgiven,
> and whose sins are covered; blessed is the man
> against whom the Lord will not count his sin.
>
> —Romans 4:7–8

What is lawlessness?

_____

_____

_____

_____

What does it mean to be covered?

_____

_____

_____

_____

Lawlessness means to be rebellious or to perform an illegal act. When we think of God's laws, we think of the Ten Commandments. Rebelliousness can also be caused when we don't follow the personal leading of the Holy Spirit. The still small voice inside of us may direct us to do something in particular that we might ignore because it makes us uncomfortable, it gives us an uneasy feeling, or we believe we can't or shouldn't do it.

The covering for our rebelliousness is the blood of Christ. The covering (roof, ceiling, awning, tent, shield, umbrella) is for protection. God's name, Jehovah-Nissi, means God is victor, banner, or protection. The blood of Christ must be visible when God looks at us to remind him that the price for our sins is paid in full. He loves to be reminded that Christ won the victory over hell and death. It pleased God to crush his son on our behalf as a guilt offering so that he, who had no earthly children, would have spiritual offspring (Isa. 53:10). His pleasure was not sadistic in nature, but God is omniscient, and he knew the end result. He was in anguish while Jesus was tortured and then hung on the cross. Yet He was pleased to save those of us who were perishing.

Day 11

> And the prayer of faith will save the one who is sick, and the Lord will raise him up. And if he has committed sins, he will be forgiven.
>
> —James 5:15

Why would a sick person need forgiveness?

_____

_____

_____

_____

Do people become sick because they sin?

_____

_____

_____

_____

The Scriptures tell us in numerous places that God no longer judges us when we sin. However, this Scripture makes it clear that we may still suffer earthly consequences of sin. Does every illness have a root of sin? By no means! Yet, *if* there is a sin root to the illness, it will be forgiven through the prayer of faith.

What are some examples of sickness caused by sin? Stress is the number one cause of disease in our world today. At its root is anxiety. The Bible states that anything we do that is not of faith is sin (Rom. 14:23). The Bible also states that we are not to be anxious about anything, but we are to pray, ask, and thank God (Phil. 4:6). Instead of faith, many people live in fear of others, of their circumstances, etc.

Ask God to show you areas in your life where you need forgiveness because you have contributed or directly caused harmful consequences to come on your body. This is difficult to do but will bring you great relief, and God can show you how to change your feelings, thoughts, and actions so they line up with his plan for your life. Repentance always opens the door for revival, refreshing, revelation, restoration, health, and blessing.

Day 12

> And forgive us our debts as we forgive our debtors.
>
> —Matthew 6:12

What is the significance of forgiving others before we ask for forgiveness?

_____

_____

_____

_____

When we initially cry out to the Lord for forgiveness and eternal salvation, have we already forgiven everyone who has troubled or hurt us?

_____

_____

_____

It is important to understand that our salvation is not dependent upon anything that we do. It is solely dependent upon receiving the free gift that God provided through the death of Jesus. So after we have become followers of Jesus Christ, is our forgiveness contingent upon our forgiving others first? No! When Christ saved us, it was finished. His forgiveness toward those who are following him is perpetual. Our forgiveness is only dependent upon our repentance. His grace can lead us to living more and more sinless lives and will also make us aware of our sin. Even though we know we are forgiven forever once we are in Christ, we continue to confess our sins. It means we let God know we understand that what we did or said or thought was wrong and that we are changing our minds and turning away from that type of speech, thoughts, or actions.

The idea that we are forgiven as we forgive our debtors indicates that we have all sinned and fallen short of the glory of God (Rom. 3:23). When we sin, we have "reasons" for it. Well, so does everyone else. God's Word states that excuses are not acceptable. God knew that it would be imperative for mankind to cooperate corporately, and that means forgiving one another. We are also moral and ethical role models and ambassadors of God's forgiveness to an unforgiving and unforgiven world.

Day 13

> This is the covenant that I will make with them
> after those days, declares the Lord: I will put
> my laws into their hearts, and write them on
> their minds; then he adds, I will remember their
> sins and lawless deeds no more. Where there is
> forgiveness of these, there is no longer any offering
> for sin.
>
> —Hebrews 10:16–18

What is being forgiven in the verse above?

_____

_____

_____

_____

Why is there no longer any offering needed when there is forgiveness?

_____

———————————————————————————

———————————————————————————

———————————————————————————

It was impossible for the blood of bulls and goats to completely and permanently take away sin (Heb. 10:4). The offering had to be repeated and only covered unintentional sins. Thus, the sin offering might be performed daily (Heb. 10:11), weekly on the Sabbath, monthly, during the feasts, and/or yearly depending upon the behavior of the people. The area outside of the temple must have been bloody. Another downfall of the sin offering was that sacrifices offered were a reminder to God of the sins of his people (Heb. 10:3). When Jesus Christ died for the sins of many, he eliminated the need for any more sacrifices. The reason for that was his purity and sinless life while on earth. "For by a single offering He has perfected for all time those who are being sanctified" (Heb. 10:14). The Holy Spirit bears witness to us (inside of us; Heb. 10:15). Therefore, not only are we eternally forgiven, we can have confidence to enter the holy places by the blood of Jesus (Heb. 10:19).

Day 14

> In Him we have redemption through His blood,
> the forgiveness of our trespasses, according to the
> riches of His grace.
>
> —Ephesians 1:7

What is the difference between a trespass and a sin?

_____

_____

_____

_____

What does redemption mean?

_____

_____

_____

_____

The Scripture for today addresses trespasses. What is the difference between lawlessness, trespass, and sin? First, a sin is a situational event (*hamartia* = missing the mark) that may be intentional or unintentional. Repeated sin can become a trespass (habit) over time in the form of outright rebellion, "which is as the sin of witchcraft" (1 Sam. 15:23). The difference between lawlessness and sin is that lawlessness is a trespass (or willful violation of the law) and is more serious in nature than sin because it is an act of the free will. The law that is being broken "has but a shadow of the good things to come instead of the true form of these realities, it can never, by the same sacrifices that are continually offered every year, make perfect those who draw near" (Heb. 10:1). That is why Christ's death redeemed us from the curse of the law. Redemption is trading something seemingly worthless for something of value. Jesus's blood opened for us a new and living way through the curtain (into the holy of holies of the temple), that is, through his flesh. That is, he traded his valuable flesh for our worthless sin. Not that we are worthless, only our sin nature. God still values us in Christ as worthy.

Day 15

> Bearing with one another and, if one has a
> complaint against another, forgiving each other;
> as the Lord has forgiven you, so you also must
> forgive.
>
> —Colossians 3:13

What does it mean "to bear with one another"?

_____

_____

_____

_____

What complaints do we have against one another? Are they legitimate?

_____

_____

Bearing with one another can be thought of as carrying someone else's burden of sin that was committed against us. It is "to convey or carry." It is the extension of mercy to another person that we ourselves hope to receive when we sin against God or others. It is not an option but a directive. God provided an example of true forgiveness through Jesus Christ to us. He expects us to follow his example.

What complaints do we forgive? Do we forgive just the small offenses against us, or do we forgive those we feel we can handle forgiving? No! God forgives all our sins, and we are expected to forgive all the sins committed against us. The basis of God's forgiveness is love, and our platform for forgiveness is to be love as well. We also know that when we carry the burden of sin from another person, we can give it to God, and he will then exchange it for a lighter burden that we are able to handle. We can only handle a certain amount of load at one time before we need to get it off our backs. In essence, we pass the burden of someone else's sin onto Jesus, who already died for it. This also prevents us from looking for offenses or reasons to be hurt.

Day 16

> Be kind to one another, tenderhearted, forgiving
> one another, as God in Christ forgave you.
> Therefore be imitators of God, as beloved children.
>
> —Ephesians 4:32, 5:1

How are tenderheartedness and forgiving related to one another?

_____

_____

_____

_____

How are kindness and forgiving related to one another?

_____

_____

_____

_____

The love chapter, 1 Corinthians 13, states that the gifts of the Holy Spirit lose their power and become useless if they are not used in love. In 1 Corinthians 4:4, love is defined within the Scripture itself as patient and kind. In 1 Corinthians 4:8, love is referred to as unending or eternal. This represents the Father's type of love for us. God is also described as tender and merciful (Luke 1:78). His example, again, is for our benefit. It is expected that if we represent him, we will display the same type of unending love for others that he does as our ultimate role model.

We benefit individually in that we surround ourselves with an atmosphere of love and forgiveness. We also learn to lessen our anxiety by carrying fewer burdens addressed on day 15. Finally, we please God by imitating him as well as obeying Him. Corporately, there is more peace when people forgive one another. Where there is peace, much is accomplished by the Lord's people. When the world sees our righteous behavior, it will also draw them to Christ.

Day 17

> If we confess our sins, He is faithful and just
> to forgive us our sins and cleanse us from all
> unrighteousness.
>
> —1 John 1:9

Why do we have to confess our sins if he already knows we are going to sin and which sins we will commit?

_____

_____

_____

_____

It is true that God is omniscient. He loves us and forgave us before we were born on earth, knowing full well that we would sin against him our entire lives. God loves to be reminded that he forgives us. It brings him pleasure to remember Jesus's sacrifice. We can walk in the perpetual grace and forgiveness of God while daily remembering to ask him to cleanse us from *all* sin. Once we are forgiven for a sin, God does not hold it against us. He forgets that it was ever committed.

Knowing we are forgiven does not guarantee we will not sin again. It might be an area of past vulnerability that was not resolved. It may be something we knew that we willfully, intentionally have endeavored in. Or it might be a sin new to us, and we may not have had understanding that it is sin. We may struggle with habits or addictions. By practicing a lifestyle of repentance by focusing on Jesus's death, by maintaining a good relationship with our Father God, and by living in an atmosphere of biblical forgiveness habits, we will eventually decrease the sin in our lives.

If sin has crept into our lives, we can confess it and feel the wonderful power of the cleansing flood wash over us. The blood of Jesus is an unending fountain that makes us clean, youthful, healthy, stable, prosperous, and blessed in every way.

Day 18

> If we say we have no sin, we deceive
> ourselves and the truth is not in us.
>
> —1 John 1:8

What is arrogance?

_____

_____

_____

_____

What does it mean to be deceived?

_____

_____

_____

_____

What is the danger in believing you are forgiven?

_____

_____

_____

_____

The only way a person can come to the Father for forgiveness is to truly believe that s/he is a sinner and understand that only by receiving the sacrifice Christ made by shedding his blood can the unbeliever be saved. The individual goes from unclean to clean, from unbelieving to believing, from eternal damnation to eternal life. "I call heaven and earth to witness against you today, that I have set before you life and death, blessing and curse. Therefore, choose life that you and your offspring may live" (Deut. 30:19). Christ is the only way to eternal life, and everyone is welcome!

Assurance of forgiveness should bring us joy and freedom. It is not meant to be a stumbling block over which we fall. Arrogance and self-deception can lead us further from God rather than toward him. The only true joy and freedom come from receiving his forgiveness through Christ.

Once we start to believe that it comes from ourselves, we no longer need him. Christ's sacrifice becomes useless and vain. Then we fall into the trap of living a secular form of religion that is dead. Remember, the life is in the blood.

Day 19

> I acknowledged my sin to you, and I did not
> cover my iniquity; I said, "I will confess my
> transgressions to the Lord," and you forgave the
> iniquity of my sin.
>
> —Psalm 32:5

How long does it take God to forgive us after we confess our sin?

_____

_____

_____

_____

What happens when you try to hide your sin?

_____

_____

The Scriptures clearly tell us that our sin will find us out (Num. 32:23). It doesn't say that after our conversion to Christianity that reformation will hide our sin or give us license to sin (Rom. 6:1–2). On the contrary, we who have died to sin love God so much and appreciate what Jesus Christ did for us that we want to not only live holy lives. When we initially confess our sin to God, he forgives us once and for all. Since we live in perpetual forgiveness, there is no time between our confession and his answer. We are surrounded with forgiveness if we reach out and take it. The scriptures state that we have assurance of forgiveness (1 John 5:11). There is no need to hide sin, to fear it, or to be ashamed of needing forgiveness. This also does not mean that we must spend all our time obsessing over our sin and confessing it all day long. That is the purpose of perpetual forgiveness. We can ask forgiveness for sin daily and be assured that our sins are covered by the blood of Christ throughout the day. Otherwise we are taking things too far in the opposite direction and turning our faith into a superstition. God desires that we focus on him and what he does for us rather than on ourselves and our failures; his sacrifice, not our vain attempts.

Day 20

> And whenever you stand praying, forgive, if
> you have anything against anyone, so that your
> Father also who is in heaven may forgive you your
> trespasses.

—Mark 11:25

Why does the Scripture command us to forgive others when we are praying?

_____

_____

_____

_____

Why does this Scripture seem to tell us that our forgiveness from God is dependent upon forgiving others?

_____

_____

God does not want anything or anyone standing in the way of our prayers. He desires our time with him to be focused on him and our relationship with him. If you spend time with your best friend or your beloved spouse, and all you do is recount the hurts that have been committed against you by others, the relationship will not grow. In the relationship with God, do we only talk about our problems and those who have offended us? He tells us that unforgiveness hinders us. God has been our role model of forgiveness. It is the foundation of the Christian faith. Christ forgave those who were killing him. He does not block our salvation if we have not forgiven others, but he expects us to grow in forgiveness ability. It doesn't matter if we are perfect at the art of forgiving but that we endeavor to forgive like he did. We forgive whether we feel like it or not, and then the act of forgiveness opens the doors for the feelings to follow. It all happens in the spiritual realm, which is unseen. It will later manifest itself in the natural, seen world.

Day 21

> You forgave the iniquity of your people;
> you covered all their sin.
>
> —Psalm 85:2

Who are God's people?

_____

_____

_____

_____

What does "you covered all their sin" mean?

_____

_____

_____

_____

On day 4, the difference between sin and iniquity was presented. Sin (*hamartia*) is a situational event whereas iniquity is perversion. Sin, when repeated long-term, can alter our DNA/RNA and become iniquity. Jesus forgave the long-term, perverse iniquity; he covered all our sin. Forgiveness means that anything owed to the offended person is renounced. The debt is paid. We owe God nothing for our perversions and continued disobedience. When God covered our sin, he put a veil between that sin and his eyes. Instead of seeing our wickedness, after we accept Christ as our savior, the Father sees only the righteous blood of Christ covering us like a cloak or shield. "Blessed is the man whose transgression is forgiven, whose sin is covered" (Ps. 32:1).

This verse also assures us, again, that all our sin is covered. The sin does not live outside of us. In the natural realm, we are covered in it like a cloak. That is why God recovers us with the blood of his son, Jesus Christ. So every act we commit that is abhorrent to him is still wrong, but *we* are forgiven. God does not forgive the act, he forgives the offender. When someone offends or hurts us, we forgive the person while the action or behavior was still wrong. If we focus on forgiving the person like God focuses on forgiving us, we begin to understand how love covers each offender.

Day 22

> And out of pity for him, the master of that servant
> released him and forgave him the debt.
>
> —Matthew 18:27

What is a debt?

_____

_____

_____

_____

Who forgave the debt?

_____

_____

_____

_____

What does it mean to take pity on someone?

_____

_____

_____

_____

When we make Jesus the Lord of our lives, we are in essence saying that we make God our master. We are his servants. If we are his servants, we are blessed because he is the only one who truly has the power and authority to forgive us when we sin. Many individuals see debt as purely sin debt. They believe that financial debt is sin because it gives someone else power over your life. Financial debt was also cancelled at the cross. The blood, symbolized by the wine consumed for Communion, not only covers our sin nature, it also covers financial debt owed to institutions or people.

When you take Communion, thank God for forgiving your sin nature, your sins of commission, your sins of omission, and your financial debts as well. Jesus took pity on you at the cross. He did not just sympathize with you, but he felt the effects of your sins in his body, his mind, and his spirit. He can now empathize with you.

Day 23

> Two others, who were criminals were led away to
> be put to death with him. And when they came
> to the place that is called The Skull, there they
> crucified Him, and the criminals, one on His
> right and one on His left. And Jesus said, "Father,
> forgive them, for they know not what they do."
>
> —Luke 23:34

Who was asking for forgiveness in this verse?

_____

_____

_____

_____

To whom was the forgiveness request made?

_____

_____

In this verse, Jesus was asking the Father to forgive those who assisted in his death. He had not yet completed the work at Calvary, and salvation could not come through him. His request was made to his Father, who was the one demanding payment for sin. He spoke these words aloud so that those around him could know who his father was, who had the power to forgive sins, and that he had an intimate relationship with God. His use of the word *Father* in Hebrew is Abba or "daddy." It indicates a close family relationship and is possible only with the Holy Spirit (Gal. 4:6).

Since Christ's death, we have the right to call on our "Abba" or "daddy" in an intimate way. We ask God to forgive us, not because we offer the blood of animals or because we can make up for our sins, but because of the shed blood of Jesus Christ. So we pray for forgiveness to the Father in the name and finished work of Christ. Only the risen Christ sits at the Father's right hand in heaven, interceding for us (Rom. 8:34). Not receiving forgiveness because we feel unworthy or want to atone for ourselves is also an insult. The greatest sin is to reject Christ.

Day 24

> Judge not, and you will not be judged; condemn
> not, and you will not be condemned; forgive, and
> you will be forgiven.

—Luke 6:37

When you forgive, who will forgive you?

_____

_____

_____

_____

Notice in the above verse that forgiveness is associated with judgment and condemnation. If we read the following verse, it states that when you "give it will be given to you, pressed down, shaken together will men give into your bosom." This is an indication that we are more willing to forgive those who have forgiven or are willing to forgive us. We tend to judge and condemn people. There are people who will forgive you because some individuals have a natural gift to forgive and tenderheartedness for forgiving. Others will hold unforgiveness against you. Yet, how could we withhold forgiveness from others when we are forgiven by God himself as well as others? Since God has forgiven your offenders, you don't have the supernatural, legal right to withhold forgiveness either. It only hurts you, not the offender.

The only way we can possibly have the strength to forgive others is by the Holy Spirit, who came to live inside of you the moment you received Jesus as your Lord and Savior. One of his jobs is to convict us of sin, righteousness, and judgment (John 16:8). He washes and renews us (Titus 3:5). He reveals the deep things of God to us (1 Cor. 2:10), like how to forgive. He dispenses God's love into our hearts (Rom. 5:5). We know love led God to forgive us. One of the most important things he does is empower us (Luke 4:14, 24:49; Rom. 15:19; Acts 1:8).

Day 25

> Please pardon the iniquity of this people, according
> to the greatness of your steadfast love, just as you
> have forgiven this people, from Egypt until now.
>
> —Numbers 14:19

Who was asking for the forgiveness?

_____

_____

_____

_____

Who was being forgiven?

_____

_____

_____

_____

The intercessor here was Moses, who was interceding for the Hebrews after they had grumbled against Moses and Aaron during their sojourn in the wilderness. Notice that Moses was able to intercede for an entire nation or body of people. This is an example to us today about praying for our nation and all the nations of the world. Also note how Moses organized his prayer. He asked respectfully (please) for God to pardon the people. He then reminded God of his steadfast (unmoving) love for the Jewish people. He also reminded God that He had freed the people from oppressive slavery in Egypt and stated that he understood God had not only freed them, but was still protecting them in the present time.

When we intercede for nations, we can use the same format. We approach God with respect, reverence, and the honor due to him. We can remind God of what he has done in the past for nations such as showing mercy, creating revival, and rescuing people both spiritually and in the natural realm. It also pleases him when we recount how he rescued his chosen people from the Egyptians. We then ask him to forgive the nation we are praying for and ask him to show us specific things we can repent of for those nations. Examples of sin within nations is legislative, judiciary, financial, military, moral, ethical, spiritual, demonic, sexual, marital, academic, etc. Pray on behalf of your nation.

Day 26

> Who is a God like You, pardoning iniquity and
> forgiving transgression for the remnant of His
> inheritance? He does not retain His anger forever,
> because He delights in steadfast love. He will again
> have compassion on us; He will tread our iniquities
> underfoot. You will cast all our sins into the depths
> of the sea.
>
> —Micah 7:18–19

Who is being pardoned in the scripture?

_____

_____

_____

_____

What will happen after the forgiveness? What is the exchange?

_____

_____

_____

_____

What happens to the iniquities, transgressions, and sins?

_____

_____

_____

_____

The forgiveness in this verse is a reminder to God that there is no being greater than him. He is reminded that he alone has loved so much that he pardoned iniquity, transgression, and sin. He has pardoned a remnant of people from Israel and Judah. Even though it was a very small group, he was still willing to pardon them. He was reminded that his love was firm and unending, and that although he was angry, it did not last forever. He is an all-consuming fire (Deut. 4:24, Heb. 12:29) and can destroy every created being throughout eternity if he would not hold. Instead, he treads the iniquities of the people underfoot and casts all the sins of the people into the depths of the sea. In that way, God's justice is served as well as his love for his chosen ones.

Day 27

> To the Lord our God belong mercy and
> forgiveness, for we have rebelled against Him.
>
> —Daniel 9:9

Who receives the honor in this scripture?

_____

_____

_____

_____

What does it mean that "to God belongs forgiveness"?
Does God need forgiveness?

_____

_____

_____

_____

Who had rebelled against the Lord?

_____

_____

_____

_____

Unless you read this verse carefully, you might misinterpret it. When it states that "to the Lord our God belong mercy and forgiveness," it is difficult to tell if God needs mercy and forgiveness. Never! When you read to the end of the verse, it completes the thought by indicating that the people had rebelled against God, and they owed him forgiveness and required his mercy.

This is another instance in which a single individual interceded and asked forgiveness for a nation. In the verses just preceding this one, Daniel prayed after having a disturbing vision and a brief illness due to it. He began his prayer with reverence by telling God how awesome he was. He then proceeded to remind God of his firm, unending love. He then reported the wrongdoing of the people who had acted wickedly, by breaking God's commandments and rules, and rebelling. God's very own people had rebelled against him again. Chapter 9 of Daniel is an excellent template for a prayer for the nations. An intercessor can insert the nation's name in place of Jerusalem or Israel since every nation on earth had sinned against God and requires forgiveness.

Day 28

> Help us, O God of our salvation, for the glory of
> your name; deliver us and forgive our sins for Your
> name's sake.

—Psalm 79:9

Why would God forgive us for his sake?

_____

_____

_____

_____

Is God's reputation at stake in this scripture? No! The individual praying was pleading with God to forgive the people so that the whole earth would see God's goodness through his forgiveness. It is appropriate to pray for God to be glorified in the earth and for unbelievers to see how God treats those who trust in him. Why would anyone want to come to the saving knowledge of Jesus Christ only to find that God forces her/him into a life of suffering, misery, and hardship? It is better that the world see how much God loves those of us who have eternal life in Christ, and that even though we face difficulties, he delivers us out of them all (Ps. 34:19).

It is also an example to the world that we sin and are forgiven time and time again. God is the one who shows himself faithful (Ps. 18:25) in keeping his word. As God is faithful in forgiving, the world also needs to see his followers being faithful in forgiving. When we believe we can't do it, it is his Holy Spirit that enables us to do all things (Phil. 1:19). The world will know we are his followers when our character reflects him, and forgiveness unlocks the doors that have been held shut in the spiritual realm. We forgive when we don't feel like it because God commands us to do it. In the end, when we freely give the gift of forgiveness to someone, we receive the benefit of doing so, and we represent God in the earth in the positive light.

Day 29

> For your name's sake, O Lord,
> pardon my guilt, for it is great.
>
> —Psalm 25:11

Who is asking for forgiveness?

_____

_____

_____

_____

Who is benefitting from the forgiveness?

_____

_____

_____

_____

Why is God being entreated to protect his name's sake?

_____

_____

_____

_____

Why did the psalmist state that his sin was "great"?

_____

_____

_____

_____

The psalmist was pleading with God to forgive him to uphold his (God's) reputation in the earth. The author did not merit God's forgiveness through any means of his own. He didn't earn God's forgiveness, and his prayer was a sign of humility. When a servant (and we are God's servants) disobeyed his master, the consequences could be severe. The plea was for mercy to wipe out the debt owed to God for gross disobedience. We know the rules we are to live by, and yet we will still think for ourselves when we know that God has already provided the answer. We will still go down the path we choose when God has already chosen a path for us. We will give our human opinions on matters rather than stating what God wants us to say. We will adopt thoughts and attitudes contrary to God's will. In this instance, the Psalmist understood how holy God was, how immense his own disobedience was, and that God had every legal right to punish him severely. His plea for God to forgive him so that he, God, would benefit was fitting.

Day 30

> Then hear from heaven your dwelling place and
> forgive and render to each whose heart you know,
> according to all his ways, for you, you only, know
> the hearts of the children of mankind.
>
> —2 Chronicles 6:30

Who was asking to be forgiven?

_____

_____

_____

_____

Other than forgiveness, what was part of the request?

_____

_____

_____

King Solomon was asking God to bless the people and the temple. He could not forget to ask God to forgive himself and the people. God did not want his people to build a temple or to put a man in authority over them. He made this clear to Solomon's father, David. Yet the people cried out for it. They also continued to disobey God in many other ways. King Solomon was asking God to give the people a second chance.

He also asked God to reward those people whose hearts were truly for the Lord. He reminded God that no man could judge that but only God himself. This was the time before Christ came to earth and people had to live a pure life to please God. When they didn't, the sacrifice of animals was necessary to atone for sin. Yet God is aware that some of Jesus's followers are wholeheartedly seeking after him and want to do that which pleases him. Believers will not be judged in heaven about eternal life. We will be judged for the deeds we have performed on earth in his name, or through error and selfishness. If we follow him even when it seems wrong, he will bless our obedience.

Day 31

> And the priest shall make atonement for him
> with the ram of the guilt offering before the Lord
> for his sin that he has committed, and he shall be
> forgiven for the sin that he has committed.
>
> —Leviticus 19:22

Why was the priest responsible for making the sin offering on behalf of the individual?

_____

_____

_____

_____

How many people did the priest atone for each day, week, month, and year?

_____

_____

The high priest and his aides were the only ones who were allowed to offer sacrifices before God because they were consecrated in special ceremonies for their posts. They also had strict rules to live and work by to please a holy God. The temple was like a slaughterhouse because the priests were covered in blood on a daily basis as they made the sacrifices for the entire nation. There were also many different types of offerings (burnt, peace, sin, guilt, the red heifer, and food and drink). The priests were also required to eat parts of the animals sacrificed (mainly the fat and protein) and were reported to have excruciating indigestion in ancient Hebrew writings.

It is now a monumental relief that Jesus Christ performed all the work for the priests for all mankind for all eternity. No more will the people of God have to wallow in the blood of animals, for his blood covered every sin. God commands us to remember his son's sacrifice by taking Communion. It is a small request in exchange for eternal life.

REFERENCES

Beck, Aaron, and Brad Alford. "Cognition and Psychopathology." *In Depression: Causes and Treatment.* 2nd ed. Philedelphia, Pennsylvania: University of Pennsylvania Press, 2009.

Berry, Jack et al., "Forgivingness, Vengeful Rumination, and Affective Traits." *Journal of Personality* 73, no. 1 (2005): 183–225.

Brown, Ryan. "Vengeance is mine: Narcissism, vengeance, and the tendency to forgive." *Journal of Research in Personality* 38 (2004): 576–584.

Corey, Gerald. *Theory and Practice of Counseling and Psychotherapy.* 7th ed. Belmont, CA: Brooks/Cole-Thomson Learning, 2005.

Corsini, Raymond J, and Danny Wedding. *Current psychotherapies.* 8th ed. Belmont, CA: Brooks/Cole-Thomson Learning, 2010.

Covenant. (n.d.). In *BibleGateway.com*. Accessed June 28, 2012.

Einstein, Albert. "Science, Philosophy and Religion: A Symposium." 1939.

Ellis, Albert. "Early Theories and Practices of Rational Emotive Behavior Theory and How They Have Been Augmented and Revised During the Last Three Decades. *Journal of Rational-Emotive and Cognitive-Behavior Therapy* 21, no. 3–4. (2003).

Farrow, Tom et al.,. "Quantifiable Change in Functional Brain Response to Empathic and Forgivability Judgments with Resolution of Posttraumatic Stress Disorder." *Psychiatry Research: Neuroimaging* 140, (2005): 45–53.

Farrow, Tom et al., "Investigating the Functional Anatomy of Empathy and Forgiveness." *NeuroReport* 12, no. 11 (2001): 2433–2438.

Jack, Rachael, Oliver Garrod, and Philippe Schyns. "Dynamic Facial Expressions of Emotion Transmit an Evolving Hierarchy of Signals over Time." *Current Biology* 24, no. 2 (2014): 187–92. Accessed May 26, 2015. doi:10.1016/j.cub.2013.11.064.

Johnston, Sandra. *The effects of forgiveness therapy and narrative therapy training with graduate counseling students: Personal, academic, and professional development, and personal well-being.* Published doctoral dissertation, University of Wisconsin, Madison, 2011.

Johnston, Sandra. *The effects of forgiveness on the symptoms of posttraumatic stress disorder as a result of sexual trauma.* Published master's thesis, University of Wisconsin, Whitewater, 2007.

Kalish, Charles, and Lawson Chris. "Negative Evidence and Inductive Generalization." *Thinking & Reasoning* 13, (2007): 394–425.

Kubzansky, Laura, and Ichiro Kawachi. "Going to the Heart of the Matter: Do Negative Emotions Cause Coronary Heart Disease?" *Journal of Psychosomatic Research 48,* no. 4–5 (2000): 323–37. Accessed May 26, 2015. doi:10.1016/S0022-3999(99)00091-4.

Linehan, Marsha. *Cognitive Behavioral Treatment of Borderline Personality Disorder.* New York: Guilford Press, 1993.

Luskin, Frederic Karni Ginzburg, and Carl Thoresen. "The Effect of Forgiveness Training on Psychosocial Factors in College Age Adults." *Humboldt Journal of Social Relations. Special Issue: Altruism, intergroup apology and forgiveness: antidote for a divided world* 29, no. 2 (2005): 163–184. Print.

Noll, Jenny. "Forgiveness in people experiencing trauma." In *Handbook of Forgiveness,* edited by Everett Worthington, Jr., 363–376. New York: Brunner-Routledge, 2005.

Orathinkal, Jose and Alfons Vansteenwegen. "The Effect of Forgiveness on Marital Satisfaction in Relation to Marital Stability." *Contemporary Family Therapy: An International Journal* 28, no. 2 (2006): 251–260.

Roberts, Robert C. "Forgivingness." *American Philosophical Quarterly* 32, (1995): 289–306.

Steadfast. (n.d.). In *Merriam-Webster.com*. Web. Accessed June 28, 2012.

Strong, James. *The New Strong's Complete Dictionary of Bible Words*. Nashville; Thomas Nelson, 2010.

Toussaint, Loren, and Jon Webb. "Gender Differences in the Relationship Between Empathy and Forgiveness. *The Journal of Social Psychology*, 145, no. 6, (2005): 673–685. Print.

Tugade, Michele, Barbara Fredrickson, and Lisa Feldman-Barrett. "Psychological Resilience and Positive Emotional Granularity: Examining the Benefits of Positive Emotions on Coping and Health." *Journal of Personality*, 72, no. 6 (2004): 1161–190. Accessed May 26, 2015. doi:10.1111/j.1467-6494.2004.00294.x.

Uchino, Bert, Timothy Smith, Julianne Holt-Lunstad, Rebecca Campo, Maija Reblin. "Stress and Illness." In *Handbook of Psychophysiology*, edited by John Cacioppo, Louis Tassinary, and Gary Berntson, 608–632. 3rd ed. New York: Cambridge University Press, (2007).

Wade, Nathaniel and Everett Worthington, Jr. "Overcoming interpersonal offenses: Is forgiveness the only way to deal with unforgiveness?" *Journal of Counseling & Development,* 81, (2003): 343–353. Print.

Witvliet, Charlotte. "Forgiveness and psychophysiology: Four experiments emphasizing emotion." Paper presented at the 6th Annual Meeting of the Society for Personality and Social Psychology, New Orleans, LA, January 2005.

Witvliet, Charlotte, Thomas Ludwig, and Kelly Vander Laan. "Granting Forgiveness or Harboring Grudges: Implications for Emotions, Physiology, and Health." *Psychology Science,* 121, no. 2 (2001): 117–123. Print

Witvliet, Charlotte, Kelly Phipps, Michelle Feldman, and Jean Beckham, "Posttraumatic Mental and Physical Health Correlates of Forgiveness and Religious Coping in Military Veterans." *Journal of Traumatic Stress,* 17, no. 3 (2004): 269–273. Print.

Woolf, H. B. (Ed.). *Webster's New Collegiate Dictionary.* Springfield, MA: G. & C. Merriam Company. 1980.

Worthington Jr., Everett. *Five steps to forgiveness: The art and science of forgiving.* New York: Crown Publishers. 2001.

Worthington Jr., Everett. *Handbook of Forgiveness.* New York, NY: Brunner-Routledge. 2005.

Worthington, Jr., Everett Charlotte Witvliet, Pietro Pietrini, and Andrea Miller. Forgiveness, health, and well-being:

Sandra K. Johnston PhD, LP

A review of evidence for emotional versus decisional forgiveness, dispositional forgivingness, and reduced unforgiveness. *Journal of Behavioral Medicine,* 30, no. 4 (2007): 291–302. doi: 10.1007/s10865–007–9105–8.